Sycamore Mill

Also by Brad G. Leech

Sycamore Glen

Sycamore Mill

Brad G. Leech

2020

Copyright © 2020 by Brad G. Leech

All rights reserved. This book or any portion thereof may not be reproduced or used in any manner whatsoever without the express written permission of the publisher except for the use of brief quotations in a book review or scholarly journal.

If this material is in the form of an eBook, it is licensed for your personal enjoyment only. This eBook may not be re-sold or given away to other people. If you would like to share this book with another person, please purchase an additional copy for each recipient. If you're reading this book and did not purchase it, or it was not purchased for your use only, then please return to your favorite eBook retailer and purchase your own copy. Thank you for respecting the hard work of this author.

ISBN 978-0-9987497-3-0 Paperback
ISBN 978-0-9987497-4-7 Hardcover
ISBN 978-0-9987497-5-4 eBook

Although every precaution has been taken to verify the accuracy of the information contained herein, the author and publisher assume no responsibility for any errors or omissions. No liability is assumed for damages that may result from the use of information contained within.

The characters, places and events in this novel are fictional. Everything has been invented, except for several commonplace items during the period this novel is set in, as well as references to various Civil War battles and several well-known soldiers from both sides of the war.

Cover design by Brad Leech

Book design by Brad Leech

Front cover photograph by Brad Leech
Sycamore over "Burnside Bridge", Antietam Creek, Sharpsburg Maryland

Printed and Bound in the United States of America

4 3 2 1

First Edition First Printing: November 2020
Published by Brad Leech
Email: bgleech1@verizon.net

For my mother,

Viola B. Daignault
1923 – 1981

My mother Vi has been gone for a while, but it hasn't been so long ago that I don't remember her smile and the twinkle in her eyes.

~ Acknowledgements ~

    This book would not have been possible without the help of my wife Connie, as a collaborator, that I relied heavily on to keep my writing moving along. This was not an easy story to put together. The concept seemed simple enough, but executing it was far more difficult than I expected it to be.

    She was my chief reader and critic as I experimented with the format of the story. I appreciate her ability to continue to read and re read my rough material and forge ahead as if she did not know what lay ahead for the characters.

~ Contents ~

Preface	3
Prologue	5
Sycamore Mill	7
Epilogue	313
Characters	315
Afterword	317
Sycamore Secrets	319
About the Author	323

~ Preface ~

This story is pure fiction. It is based on characters created in my previous writing effort, Sycamore Glen, which I wanted to expand upon. I felt that developing a story based on some of the actions of the ancestors of the residents of 'present day' Jasper might be an interesting approach to continue writing about the Glen. I've tried to uniformly space the jumps 'back in time', to hopefully, keep the main story line intact and readable. As I worked on the material that occurs a hundred years earlier, I was tempted by the idea of expanding it and keeping it a separate story, but I kept coming back to Sycamore Glen, and in the end, I have decided to keep the two stories woven together – as I originally planned.

I should also say, that since this is very much a continuation of the Sycamore Glen story, I would recommend that you read it before reading Sycamore Mill. By reading Sycamore Glen first, you'll have the complete story behind many of the characters in Sycamore Mill. I have tried to write Sycamore Mill in such a manner that reading the earlier novel is not a necessity, but I think you'll enjoy this story more if you read Sycamore Glen first.

While I've come to enjoy the writing effort, and hopefully this shows in my work - please try to look beyond any minor technical errors that may have slipped by me while editing and publishing my own material.

I hope you like the story, thanks for giving it a try!

Brad Leech

~ Prologue ~

No soldier goes into combat fully expecting what will occur. After all the drills, after all the practice, after all the team building, and after all the marksmanship lessons – war takes its own course. To a large extent, each man takes on war by himself, up close – personal. He creates his own destiny, or maybe something approaching it, each time he pulls the trigger.

There is no glory in it, it just is what it is, in that moment.

People may say afterwards that his actions were heroic, that he deserved to be recognized for accomplishing this or that. They might pin medals on his chest, honor him with parades and when he's gone, a statue. But all he did was try to survive, trying to keep the men around him alive, so that they, like him, could go on pulling the trigger again, and again ... Is that heroism?

Amidst the carnage of war, people need heroes. When one doesn't seem to exist ...

October 1859

Henry came through the area like many others. Pushed off the family farm by older siblings, he was forced to strike off on his own. He headed west, like other young farmers, to try to make a new life for himself. All he could do was offer a full days' work in exchange for meals, a place to sleep, and maybe a little money. He hoped, in time, he could become a sharecropper. He would then be able to truly profit from his efforts and perhaps start a family.

All he had to his name was a mule that had seen better days. Henry had farmed with the mule at home. When he left, there was no debating that the mule would leave with him. The problem was that the mule liked Henry – and no one else. The two worked long hours together and were accustomed to each other's temperament. Right now, Jack wanted to stop and have a drink of water from the stream he'd spotted nearby. Henry was thirsty also. He too had noticed the stream tumbling down the hillside and nudged Jack in that general direction.

He had Jack pull up beneath a towering sycamore that arched out over the stream. He jumped to the ground and let Jack wander into the water, then walked upstream a couple of paces and knelt to drink the water. It was cold and quenched his thirst quickly. When he was finished, he looked over at Jack, the mule had also finished drinking and was just standing in the water.

The two of them looked out into the valley that was spread out below them. There were a couple of farms established in the bottom of the valley, probably along a larger creek. He'd passed through a small village a couple of days before and was told that there were some farms in the next settlement, west of there. The town was called Jasper.

Now what kind of name was Jasper for a town? He and Jack had mulled over that question all morning. While Henry discussed the pros and cons of Jasper being a good name, Jack listened closely. In the end, Jack had to agree with Henry that Jasper was as good a name as any for a small town. Henry was always patient with Jack, the two never rushed into anything without thinking it through carefully.

The land certainly looked like it would be good for farming. Not as flat as some parts that he'd passed through recently, but still, good land. He'd need to find work soon; his money was starting to run out. Jack was having to browse for food and Henrys' supplies had dwindled. He was now hunting for each meal. He was a good shot, so he wouldn't starve, but he needed other provisions. Jack needed some proper feed and they both needed a little rest. They had been traveling almost non-stop for the last two weeks.

Henry called Jack back out of the water. He wanted to make it into Jasper by nightfall. He started walking west with Jack by his side. He'd give him a break from the additional weight for the next hour or so.

~

When they arrived in Jasper later that afternoon, they went straight to a stable. The rates were reasonable, so he boarded Jack there. Jack would get several good meals and a stable hand would give him a grooming after scrubbing him down. Henry cautioned the boy - Jack was a bit of a nipper and he should stay alert when handling his flanks at all. The boy thanked him for the warning and led Jack through into the yard behind the stable where he could wet the animal down.

Henry left the stable and walked across the street to what looked like the only dry goods store in town. He bought some small quantities of coffee, sugar, salt and some other things he'd run low on. As he paid the clerk, he asked about finding work in Jasper.

"So, Mr. Bartlett, do you know of any farmers looking for help?"

"Well son, there are a couple around here that are stretched thin right now. Let me think on it for a minute."

The storekeeper was wrapping up the purchases in an oilcloth and string, knotting it, so it would stay sealed.

"You know," he said, "there's a farmer up on Sycamore Hill - Ezekiel Jennings. He's got a big place up there. Problem is, he has no sons, just two daughters. Twins. One of 'ems married. But I don't know how much work her husband does on the farm. They're pretty private up there. Ezekiel, he's usually looking for some help. His farm would be a good place to start asking. What'd you say your name was?"

"Henry sir, Henry Hawkins. Say, do you have a newspaper? I've lost touch with what's been going on since I got on the road."

"Sure Henry, here's one. It's not local. Someone passing through a couple of days ago, left it. Just take it. Our paper, The Gazette, only comes out on Fridays."

Henry took the sheet of paper from him and looked at the headlines.

"Harpers Ferry Under Siege"

Henry looked up, "What's this all about?"

The storekeeper glanced at the paper. "It's all over with. Troops under Colonel Lee came in and recaptured the arsenal.

They've got that lunatic Brown and his sons. They're going to put him on trial – probably hang 'em all."

~ *November 5, 1859* ~

This young, lanky farmer came to the farm last week looking for work. His name is Henry Hawkins. Dad hired him - mainly because he had a mule with him. He seems nice enough, he works hard. Maybe he will last longer than the others.

Today it rained almost all-day long. I wanted to walk in the woods, but it was just too cold and wet. The water is probably roaring over the waterfall further down in the glen.

More and more of the darker bark has come off the sycamores revealing the lighter shades of green and white bark beneath. Surly this is a sign that winter is coming.

~ 1 ~

During the winter months, the construction business slowed to the point that you wondered why you ever decided to get into it. This winter was no different. Fortunately, there had been more than enough work earlier in the year to carry him through to next spring – at least financially speaking. He was used to budgeting his money to avoid serious problems during the winter lull in work. The problem this winter was that he was bored with the string of small repair jobs he'd taken on and was angry that he hadn't been able to line up a larger, continuous, job that would have at least kept him indoors. The winter had been brutal this year so far, and the Farmers' Almanac did not predict anything changing in the foreseeable future.

Chip Connors was a cabinet maker by trade but had recently been doing mostly finish work on new homes. The new construction business in Jasper had been good over the past several years and showed no signs of dropping off. His skills were well known, he had no trouble finding work – during the construction season.

He was surprised when he got the phone call from Dick Taylor asking Chip to meet him up at the clubhouse for the Sycamore Glen golf course. Chip knew that Dick did not have a lot going on and had planned on taking a break during the winter. His construction company had been going non-stop since the start of the construction boom in Jasper. He assumed this would be a business lunch to discuss a project Dick would start on in the spring. Chip was wrong.

When he pulled into the parking lot at the golf course, he was surprised to see so many vehicles. The course was closed until the spring but there were an awful lot of cars here. The pub at the course, MacGregor's, stayed open all year, but during the winter the business was always slow. Whenever Chip had come up here, at this time of the year, during the day, there were usually no more than a dozen cars in the lot.

He parked and made his way into the clubhouse. When he came through the doorway he was met by Curtis Aldridge, the club manager, who was expecting him, and guided him into MacGregor's. It looked as though everyone that had parked outside was in MacGregor's. The tables in the pub had been re arranged into a horseshoe shape to accommodate the twenty people, or so, that were standing about in several small groups talking amongst themselves.

When Dick saw Chip enter, he mentioned this to the person he was talking to that had his back to the doorway. They could begin now, everyone was here. Dan Steele, the course owner, turned to face Chip, "Come on in Chip, take a seat. We'll get started now that you're here."

Chip pulled a chair away from the table and sat down next to Dick. Dick leaned in close to him and said, "I didn't want to scare you away from this by telling you too much on the phone."

Dan remained standing. He started out, "I think we all know each other here, so I won't dwell on any formalities. We've got some ideas on changing the clubhouse around a bit and we thought we'd invite some of you up here to see if you could help us out. Ian, you jump in here anytime if you think it's necessary. Mary, Cletus, you too."

Ian MacGregor was the owner of the pub/restaurant at the Sycamore Glen golf course – MacGregor's. While Ian tended bar, his daughter Mary essentially ran MacGregor's. She was seated beside her father, and next to her, sat her husband, Cletus. He had come into the community several years before in the company of Dan Steele – who now owned the golf course. When Cletus had met the auburn-haired Mary, he knew his world had changed forever. When offered work at the course, he had never asked about the pay – he would have stayed no matter what was offered.

Ian nodded for Dan to continue. Mary and Cletus stayed quiet.

Dan continued, "Most of you have been up here for golf or dinner and I think you can probably see that we're a bit cramped for space. Speaking about the golf side of the business, we need more room in both the pro shop and downstairs in the locker room. Over the past couple years, well … we've outgrown the room we have in here. We could also use some more office space."

Dan nodded to Mary, who stood up and said, "Here in the pub we don't have room to turn around, and we desperately need more kitchen space. I think that those of you that have eaten here recently have noticed that there is usually a waiting line to be seated. We just aren't comfortable with that situation. Dick is a family friend and we've talked with him about this problem for quite a while now. He suggested we ask all of you up here to listen to some ideas we have about what we could do with the clubhouse. MacGregor's and the golf course are separate businesses, but obviously, we're closely connected and what happens with one will affect the other."

Dan stood back up, "Thanks Mary. We know you all have experience in different fields – plumbing, masonry, electrical and so on. We haven't drawn up specific plans yet, but if you'll listen to some of our ideas, we'd appreciate it. We'll be looking for your expertise to carry out what we decide to do."

Dan continued, "In talking with Dick we realized that all of you have busy schedules during the warmer months. During those same months, we're busiest here. MacGregor's is open all year, so a big part of our plan is to avoid too much disruption concerning the pub. In talking with Dick, he stressed that putting together a work schedule, coordinating a wide variety of activities coupled with business demands of both the course and MacGregor's, would be crucial. When I offered Dick the job, he was grateful, but turned me down – like I knew he would. What he offered, however, was a recommendation that I bring in Chip Connors, over here, as a project manager for the duration of the construction."

Chip had been listening but didn't realize that Dan was talking about him for several moments. When he did, he was shocked.

Dan continued, "Chip, I didn't want to hit you with the job like this, but Dick said you'd probably turn it down unless you understood what we're trying to accomplish."

Chip said, "Dan, Dick was right. I'm no project manager. I'm flattered you thought of me, but I'm just a cabinet maker."

Dan said, "Well that's just it Chip, that's exactly what I think we're looking for here. We need someone to piece together a lot of activities, probably in a manner that most contractors would have a tough time with. Dick and I know that the people in this room have the skills to accomplish all this. But with all the work you all normally do; it may be hard for us to get onto your schedules. We realize that this work would be in addition to what you normally do. It's not like we expect to get all this done overnight."

Dan looked at Chip, "So what do you think? You'd be a full-time employee here. Dick and I have estimated this would take at least three years, but that's just a rough guess. A lot will depend on what we come up with for the final plans."

Chip was thinking this over, still unconvinced he was the person for the job.

Dan looked around the room. "You folks think Chip would be someone you could work with to pull this off?"

There was a lot of heads nodding. Phil Jackson, a mason, stood up. "Chip, we've worked together on several jobs. I agree with Dan, you'd be great at this. As much as I'd like to get involved with this project, Dan's right. I've got work booked for quite a while. For me to get involved, I'd need to make sure things were laid out right to guarantee that my work isn't stalled out because of other work not happening on time."

Cletus had been silent during all this. As Phil sat down Cletus stood up. He said, "Chip, I haven't known you as long as your friends, here. But I've seen some of your work. I know you've used some hardwood we've taken out of the woods for some projects you've done elsewhere. You are a true craftsman. I think that what Mary, Ian and Dan have in mind here could turn out to be something special when it's all done. With your leadership, it will be something special. What do you say?"

Chip looked at Dan, was hesitant …, "Dan I'll take the job if you really think I'm the right person for it."

Dan reached out to shake Chip's hand, "You are Chip." He leaned in close and said, "We'll get along just fine. We'll work out the details. I'm sure we can agree on a salary. Stick around when this is all over with and we'll discuss everything."

Chip shook Dan's hand and thought, 'What am I getting into here?'

Dan said to everyone, "Okay, now, let's everyone get a coffee or something to drink. Settle in here, and we'll tell you about some of the things we'd like to see happen - now that we've got a manager who'll sort out all these crazy ideas and make it happen."

As the winter wore on and spring approached, Chip spent most of his time at the Sycamore Glen clubhouse. He had set up a bedroom and cleaned out a small office area in the old "mill" portion of the building. This was on the first floor, beneath Mary and Cletus' apartment. It was perfect. The area had been converted to a machine shop when the mill stopped operating, and still had some of the equipment that had been powered by the mill. The old overhead belt drive system was still pretty much intact. Some of the machinery had been sold off when the mill eventually closed, but there were still some interesting machines that he examined from time to time.

He moved a drafting table into what had once been the office for the mill and was making sketches and diagrams to incorporate the ideas that everyone at Sycamore Glen had presented at the first meeting they'd had. But it didn't stop there. There was a steady flow of thoughts about the renovations that would start happening when the plans were finalized, and the building permits taken out.

He met with Dan and Ian each morning in MacGregor's, and over breakfast, they would discuss all the latest thoughts about the changes he was going to begin to make happen.

This morning started out like others had since the snow had melted. He had walked outside the entrance to the parking area and was fascinated by the sight of the sycamores coming into full bloom. This really was a gorgeous location. When you came up the drive and made the final turn into the parking area, you were struck by the sheer beauty of the mill and the immense sycamores arching over that end of the clubhouse. There was a steady stream of water pushing past the giant wheel, cascading into several small pools that 'stair stepped' their way down the hill away from the mill. But there was something that bothered him when he saw the clubhouse as a complete building. The more recent additions really weren't in balance with the existing stone mill house. It's not that they looked bad, it's just that they looked like how they had been constructed - tacked on.

 This was on his mind as he sat down in the booth at MacGregor's next to Cletus.

 He said, "Morning Cletus. Big day ahead of you?"

 Cletus responded, "Chip, good morning. Yeah, we're going full bore out there before the season really starts up. We're getting some play, but there's still a lot to do."

 Chip continued, "Yeah, it feels like summer's not too far off by the look of the sycamores out there this morning."

 Cletus looked up as Dan came into MacGregor's and made a beeline for their booth.

 "Morning gents." Said Dan as he plopped down beside Cletus. "I see everyone is up bright and early this morning." Dan waved a hand towards Ian who was reading his newspaper at the bar. Ian nodded a silent 'good morning to you too' in return.

 Quietly Chip said to them, "There's something I need to discuss with the two of you before we all get started on other things this morning. Maybe we could step outside after breakfast, it'll only take a couple minutes."

 The words were barely out of his mouth when the kitchen door burst open and Mary came around the corner to the booth.

"Here's some breakfast." She said as she slid a plate in front of Cletus. She looked at Dan with a 'What are you having this morning? - look' on her face.

Dan responded, "Good morning Mrs. Armstrong. If it's not too much trouble, I'd like some toast with some bacon, no eggs. I'm trying to watch my weight."

She looked dubious about this statement, pointedly stepping back and staring at Dan's midsection, frowning, but said nothing. "How about you Mr. Connors? What would you like?"

Chip smiled and answered, "Just some juice and some scrambled eggs Mary. Thanks."

With that, Mary left for the kitchen.

Dan said to Cletus, "Ouch, rough night last night?"

Cletus responded, "You got that right. Katie must be coming down with a cold or something. Mary was up several times with her. She must be beat. She's hardly spoken to me this morning."

Ian had perked up at the mention of Katie's name. As much as Ian loved Mary, Mary was in danger of being replaced by Katie. Nothing the little imp ever did could get Ian angry with her. It's not that Katie was a bad child, it's just that she always had the attention of everyone around her, and she was used to getting her own way with everything she did. At least she would be going to school in another year and have the chance to be around other children. Cletus couldn't wait for that. Cletus would say she was four going on fourteen. Since all her contact was with adults, she was probably growing up faster than she would have if they lived in town where Katie would be with others her own age.

Ian came over to the booth, "Is Katie okay?"

"Sure dad, she's running a little fever, she's probably caught a cold. Mary was up with her during the night."

Mary came out of the kitchen with the meals and put them in front of Dan and Chip.

Ian said to her, "Cletus says Katie's coming down with a cold. Is she okay?"

Mary said, "She's fine dad. Like Cletus said, it's probably a cold, she'll get over it. She just had a hard time sleeping last night."

Ian said to her, "Mary, why don't you take the morning off? We can get by in here. Susan will be coming in before too much longer, we'll handle it in here. You could get a little sleep."

"You wouldn't mind dad?", questioned Mary.

"Please, leave things to us. We'll handle it. I'll explain to Susan when she gets here."

"Okay dad, you've convinced me. I've felt a little run down lately." She paused for a moment, but said, "I hope I'm not coming down with a cold. The last thing we need is to have everyone here sick."

Cletus smiled at her, "Try to get some sleep Mary."

Mary nodded to Cletus and said, "Okay then, I'll see you later, you too Dan. Chip I've got some more ideas for you. I'll catch up with you later also."

She went back to the kitchen and told Terry he was on his own until Susan showed up, then left for the apartment.

After she'd left, Chip looked around to see how busy things were in the pub. Seeing that it was fairly quiet, he asked Ian to join them before he left to return to his paper at the bar.

Chip said, "Ian, sit with us for a minute."

Ian sat down next to Dan, "What's up?"

Chip began, "I wanted to have a word with Cletus and Dan, but you should hear this too. I've been thinking about how to start the construction around here. I know we have to get started on submitting the plans to obtain the permits we'll need, but there's a problem we need to discuss before that can happen. I thought we'd discuss it before we spring this on Mary."

~ 3 ~

After their discussion, Dan asked Cletus to accompany him out onto the course. Cletus got the mowers started and had a quick chat with Tim about the spring aeration which would take place this week. It would go smoothly since Tim now had a full-time assistant to work with him on the greens. The course was in spectacular shape. With the influx of residents into Jasper and the surrounding area, the golf course had really taken off. The memberships had doubled since Dan took over the course. He had been putting most of the profits back into the course and it showed. There were many little things that Teddy and Cletus had brought to his attention about the course that, once addressed, were now paying dividends. Curtis, too, had chimed in with some ideas about the course. He had suggested they hire a professional teacher as the resident "pro" and initiate a golf training program at the club. Davis Templeton had started last year and was making a real difference at the club. They now had a steady flow of people taking lessons during the weekdays and the members enjoyed having someone to go to when they thought their golf game needed a little tweaking.

Dan and Cletus drove away from the clubhouse, up the hill towards the maintenance shed on the number 14 hole. Dan parked the cart near the shed and asked Cletus to follow him as they walked further up the hill.

"Cletus, how are things with you and Mary if you don't mind me asking?"

Cletus looked at Dan as they continued up towards the waterfall, "We're fine Dan. Mary's a little tired – and now Katie has a cold. We're fine, really."

Dan continued, "Well I was just wondering. Most times Mary seems like her old self, other times …"

Cletus looked at Dan, having a little trouble finding the right words. "I don't know Dan, sometimes it seems that there's just so much going on around Mary. You know how she is. She handles everything. Sometimes it seems like she has a little too much going on."

Dan said, "Yeah, that's what I've been wondering about too. I know with all this talk about construction and expansion at the club, maybe it's getting to her and she just isn't saying anything about it. I know she's all for the expansion of MacGregor's and what it would mean for the business, but …"

Cletus jumped in, "You've got that right, she really would like to see some of these changes happen as soon as possible." The two of them had arrived at the upper pond above the glen. Dan pointed towards the farm and the buildings on the other side of the pond. "Cletus, follow me over there."

As they approached the farmhouse Cletus saw the real estate sign out in front of the building near the driveway. Plastered over the sign was a "SOLD" sticker.

Cletus stopped and turned to face Dan, "Dan what's going on here?"

Dan smiled and said to Cletus, "You didn't know this place was up for sale did you kid? I thought I'd bring you up here and show you this before Mary found out. I know she'll probably take it pretty hard when she finds out it's been sold."

Cletus looked around at the farm. Dan was right, Mary was going to have a hard time with this. Cletus and Mary would bring

Katie up through the glen to the pond and Mary had explained to Katie that she and 'Poppy' used to live in the house on the other side of the pond. Cletus would miss the ritual of their walks around the pond to poke into the unused buildings.

Dan reached into his pocket and pulled out a set of keys, handing them to Cletus he said, "Here you go kid, I'm way ahead of Chip. I'm kicking you, Mary and Katie out of the clubhouse!"

Cletus stared down into his hand at the keys. Cletus was speechless.

"I figured that I'd let you handle this with Mary. Ian and I have talked about this for some time. He's behind me on this. We both think that maybe you and Mary need a little time and space away from the course and MacGregor's. It's not that you're so far away, but a little distance might help. You two are so wrapped up with things down there", as Dan pointed back down the hill, "you probably don't see what's happening to your family. You need this."

Cletus had collected himself, "But Dan …"

Dan said, "No buts about it. I figure you can just keep the same arrangement on the rent with the course but move up here."

Cletus still looked doubtful about this.

Dan said to him, "The truth is, I've got plans for some of the land that came with this property. It's a good deal all around. Teddy and I have been discussing adding another 18 holes to the course and turning this into a golf 'destination', we'll need more land for that. We're also thinking that we could put in a couple homes up here on the hilltop, so you wouldn't be so isolated up here. Chip doesn't know about my ideas for some homes, but he'll be busy long beyond the clubhouse renovations. Dick actually tipped me off on the property. He may buy a little of this up here from me for a couple homes he's thinking of building."

Cletus said to him, "It looks like you've thought of everything Dan."

Dan said to him, "Well there's still Mary, that's your department."

~ 4 ~

After Cletus had returned from the hilltop with Dan, he caught up with Teddy to make sure the work on the course was taking place in the way Teddy expected it to. The two of them had become a lot closer after Teddy replaced Bill Morgan as the Director of Operations at Sycamore Glen. Teddy was a more 'hands on' director than anyone expected, but the truth was, he enjoyed being outdoors and he liked working with Cletus. The feeling was mutual. If Cletus sometimes thought of Dan as a father that had been missing for so long, then Teddy could be thought of as the older brother he'd lost in Korea.

Teddy had eased back away from all the rough work on the course. Cletus could handle anything and wasn't afraid to pull in other workers to keep the course in good shape. While he once admitted that he was no golfer, you wouldn't think that if you watched him working to keep the course in pristine shape. The worst part of his job was watching some golfer take a bigger than normal divot on a shot off his fairways. If he saw you do this, he wasn't shy about instructing you on how to repair the damage. The members knew this and respected Cletus for his concern about the course.

Teddy looked up when Cletus came into his office, "Cletus, good morning. Understand you and Dan took a little field trip this morning."

Cletus dropped into a chair beside Teddy's desk, "Yeah, Dan wanted to discuss some things with me out there by the upper pond."

Teddy said, "These things wouldn't have included a discussion about a couple more holes out there to manage, would they?"

Cletus said, "As usual you're right on the mark. I understand you're thinking of another complete 18-hole course."

Teddy said, "Well, first Dan's got to acquire the property. After that, we'll need to bring an architect in here and see what he thinks about what we could do with the property. There'll be plenty of land – but laying out 18 quality holes is a whole 'nother story."

Cletus said, "Well, I'd be looking up the phone numbers of some architects, the property has a 'SOLD' sign on it right now!"

Teddy responded, "Great, now we can move ahead. I didn't want to say anything until Dan had talked to you - there's other aspects of this that he wanted to discuss with you first."

Cletus gave Teddy a concerned look, "Yeah I know. I've got to go in there," he said motioning back towards his apartment, "and bring everybody else up to speed on this."

Teddy chuckled, "Cletus, I think Mary will understand. I know she hasn't really been herself recently, but this will be okay, you'll see."

Cletus was doubtful, "Maybe, maybe not. Katie was up most of the night and Mary was with her. She went back in to try and get a little rest after breakfast. I'll be over there with her if you need me. I've got to get this over with, sooner rather than later."

Teddy said to him, "Take your time, we're caught up here for the moment. If anything comes up, I'll let you know."

Cletus got up and reluctantly left the safe haven of Teddy's office for the walk to the apartment.

January 1860

When Henry first laid eyes on Sarah Jennings he thought he'd never seen anyone as lovely as her. Her deep blue eyes, her easy-going demeanor – she drew everyone to her – like moths to a flame. Her father, Ezekiel, had made it clear from the onset that Sarah was off limits to Henry. Henry felt that he understood. He was a drifter, a nobody. What could he ever offer Sarah? He settled in at the farm and worked hard. He thought of Sarah constantly, but he didn't let it affect his work. He and Jack put in long hours in the fields around the farm atop Sycamore Hill, there were few workers that would stay long at Ezekiel's place. Ezekiel worked long hours himself and expected everyone around him to do the same. His wife was aged beyond her years, the harsh life on the farm was taking its toll on her. Their twin daughters, Sarah and Ruth worked just as hard.

Ruth had married when she turned sixteen, probably hoping to escape the farm. Her husband, Jedidiah Prescott, didn't seem cut out to be a farmer. For that matter, he didn't seem cut out to be much of anything. He went through the motions of working at the farm, but it had become obvious he would never be a success.

Sarah was still single and wouldn't duplicate her sister's mistake. When she married, it would be for love, and only love. Her father thought otherwise. Ezekiel wanted the best for his daughters. He didn't want Sarah to follow in Ruth's footsteps. He had a plan.

Ezekiel's best friend was Isaac Mueller. Isaac owned and operated a grist mill on lower sycamore pond. Isaac had only one child, a son named Josiah. Josiah had grown up with Ruth and Sarah. As children, the three of them were constant companions. Where you found one, you didn't have to look too much farther to find the other blue-eyed playmates.

Ezekiel and Isaac wanted to solidify their holdings by way of a marriage between Sarah and Josiah. On the face of things, this seemed like a good arrangement for everyone. The only problem was that Sarah wasn't sure about Josiah. As much as she liked Josiah – marriage was something else. She would never hurt his feelings by harshly rejecting him outright, but, then again, he had never asked her to marry him.

Josiah adored Sarah, but like Sarah – well ... marriage was forever.

Into this picture had strode Henry Hawkins. Sarah saw something in Henry that was absent in Josiah – and any other man she'd known. She knew what her father wanted, he made some sense, but she wasn't about to be a pawn in anyone's game.

So, everyone on Sycamore Hill tip toed around everyone else. Sooner or later something would disrupt the equilibrium.

~ *January 7, 1860* ~

I've been thinking of Josiah a great deal recently. It's no secret that father wants a marriage with Josiah to join our family with the Mueller's – really, just to join their mill with our farm. I'm sure Mr. Mueller feels the same way.

I see Henry every day and think of him also. It's likely that father has probably told him to mind himself around me. He's a hard worker, but I wonder how long he'll stay.

Cletus was formulating a plan as he made his way back through to the apartment. He quietly entered, thinking that Mary and Katie would be sleeping. He was surprised to see both in the living room. Mary had been stretched out on the sofa but, obviously, Katie was up, so Mary was up also.

Katie rushed over to see her daddy; she'd missed having breakfast with him.

Cletus said, "How's my big girl this morning? Do you feel better?"

Katie answered, "I'm still tired daddy, but I'm not sick. I wanna to go outside, but mommy says to stay in here until I feel better."

Cletus knew where this was headed, he'd played this game many times. It had been a while since he'd lost.

"Well Katie, you know your mommy is a really smart person, and she's right. When you feel better you can go outside, but not now." Cletus put his hand against her forehead, she was warm but nothing like last night. He was a little relieved.

Mary was watching, she too had taken Katie's temperature and felt that it had started to return to normal. Maybe it wasn't a cold, maybe it was something else. She did look a lot better this morning.

Cletus said to Katie, "Did you let mommy take a nap or did you keep her awake?"

Katie answered, "Mommy slept for a while but she's up now."

Mary smiled at Cletus, "I got a little sleep, I really do feel a lot better now."

'Good', thought Cletus, he said, "Are you two up for a little ride? I thought we could go up to the pond. We haven't been up there in a while."

Mary was a little suspicious, or maybe not fully awake from her nap. Katie was already running to get her jacket from her room.

As soon as she was out of sight Mary asked, "Alright, what's up?"

Cletus smiled, "I just want to take my two girls for a little ride up the hill. That's all."

Mary looked at him, "I know that smile, there's something going on here, but you don't ask that often – and Katie seems better, so let's go."

Mary and Katie waited on the patio while Cletus retrieved his cart from the maintenance shed. Mary and Katie jumped in when Cletus pulled up to get them. They were a familiar sight as they picked their way up along the creek on the edge of the course. Much like Mary when she was a young girl with her mother, Katie and Mary could often be seen in the woods near the course. Mary would miss this, once Katie started school, but for now she was enjoying the surprise family outing. They stopped at the shed near number 14 so Katie could call Curtis on the emergency telephone and let them know they were out on the course. Curtis always acted surprised when Katie called and told her to be careful and to take care of her mommy and daddy if they were with her. Like everyone else on the course, Curtis had helped raise Katie.

After they left the cart and began walking up through the woods towards the waterfall, Cletus mentioned that he was thinking of clearing out a proper path for a cart to get all the way up to the pond on top of the hill.

Mary looked and him and said, "Cletus, I don't think the course property extends all the way up to the pond. You should check where the property ends."

Cletus looked at Mary and said, "Well I don't think the new owner will care."

Mary stopped, "Cletus - the farm's been sold?"

Cletus said, "That's why I brought you out here. I wanted to tell you myself before you heard it from someone else."

Mary looked disappointed, not really upset about it. It had been over ten years since she and Ian had moved out of the farm and sold it. They were nearing the pond and Katie had raced ahead of them. Mary called out to her, "Don't play in the water, be careful."

When they reached the pond, Cletus said to her, "I didn't even know the place was for sale until Dan told me about it."

Mary nodded, "I knew it was for sale, I think Jerry is downsizing a little. He felt he had too much land to farm on his own, now that his son is gone. I hope the new owner realizes what he has here and takes care of everything. The house looks a little run down, it should be taken care of now, before it becomes a real problem."

Cletus stopped, Mary stopped too, waiting for Katie to catch up. He looked at Mary and said, "Well that's why I brought you up here. I figured you'd want to get started right away."

Mary stood looking at Cletus, not quite understanding what he'd said.

Cletus called back to Katie, "Come on Katie, let's go pick out a bedroom for you."

Katie raced up to them. "We're going to live here?"

Cletus said to her, "Well we are if it's okay with mommy. What do you think mommy?"

"Cletus, we can't afford this, can we?" Mary said quietly.

Cletus said, "Well, we can if we're renting if from the owner, and the owner is charging us same rent as he has been all along."

Mary smiled, "Dan bought the farm?"

Cletus nodded said to her, "Come on, let's catch up with Katie or she'll wind up with our bedroom!"

When the Armstrong family had come down off the hill, they came into MacGregor's to find Dan and Ian sitting at the end of the bar having coffee. Both acted as if this was just another morning at the course. Mary came up to Dan and gave him a kiss on his cheek, Katie wasn't far behind.

Dan turned to Cletus and said, "Well, I like the way you handled that!" He lifted Katie up onto her chair that sat in front of the windows where she had coloring books and crayons. He said to her, "How's my favorite little girl this morning?"

"I'm okay," she said, "I was sick last night but now I'm better!"

Dan glanced at Mary who was following the conversation, and looked back at Katie, "You look better. Your eyes are the same bright green as your mommy's this morning."

"Uncle Dan, why aren't my eyes blue like daddy's?"

Dan thought for a moment, "Well if your mommy had blue eyes then you'd have blue eyes like your mommy and daddy."

"So, my eyes are because of mommy?"

Dan explained, "Well sort of, if both your mommy and daddy had blue eyes, you'd have to have blue eyes – if either your mommy or daddy had brown eyes, you'd probably have brown eyes – but that's not the case with your mommy and daddy, so you have green eyes, they're extra special. Dan looked up at Mary with a smile." He leaned toward Mary and under his breath said, "When did you say Katie was starting school?"

Katie thought about it and continued coloring.

Ian said to Mary, "I gather that you enjoyed your trip up to the pond."

Mary said, "Yes we did. How long has this been in the works?"

Dan said, "Not that long. I think that Dick was the first person that Jerry talked to when he decided to sell. And Dick came straight to me."

Dan looked at Ian, "I know you're crowded in here with the bar business, the restaurant customers and all. But we're crowded out there." He motioned out the window to the course, "We need more room."

Ian said to him, "You really think another 18 holes is doable?"

Dan said, "Absolutely! Teddy and I have been discussing this all winter. It's going to take a year or two before it's playable. By that time, our membership will have tripled. And when you take into account all of the out-of-towners that now come here, we can't afford to not expand."

Mary looked at Cletus, he hadn't said anything in all of this. He was just looking at the excitement in Dan's face, and Ian's too. As businessmen, they were both looking forward to the challenges they would soon be facing. She made a snap decision that this was the time.

She said to Cletus, "Well all I can say mister is that you are one lucky guy."

Cletus grinned, "I've known that for some time. What makes you think I'm any luckier now?"

Mary said, "Because there's a third bedroom up there that we could never have accommodated in our apartment!"

Dan exchanged looks with Ian, they both knew instantly.

Cletus looked at Mary, "Are you expecting guests to be staying with us?"

Mary said to him, "No guests, but I am expecting."

Cletus just didn't catch on.

Dan couldn't help himself, "Hey genius, Katie's going to have a baby brother!"

Ian had never seen Cletus like this. Stunned, Cletus reached out to hug Mary and gave her a kiss.

Katie had heard her name mentioned and said to Dan, "Uncle Dan, I want a baby sister."

Dan said to her, "Well, talk this over with your mommy, maybe she can change the order before the baby gets delivered."

Katie ran across the floor towards the door. "Aunt Claire, I'm getting a baby sister, but she's going to have blue eyes!"

Everyone turned to see Claire entering MacGregor's. As Katie rushed toward her, she picked up Katie and came to the bar.

Claire said, "Well I can see that everyone here has been busy this morning! Mary, Cletus, good morning and congratulations. Ian, congratulations also. Dan, it seems you're enjoying yourself."

Dan turned to her, "That I am Mayor Steele. That I am."

Dan's brush with death in the storm that nearly destroyed the golf course several years before, had made him reevaluate much in his life. He had come face to face with death before, but this was different. He'd had more time to think things through while he was recuperating. Having already decided to purchase Judge Osborn's share of the golf course, he decided to make another big change in his life.

When he'd first met Claire, he was fascinated by everything about her. She had this controlled demeanor that just oozed confidence and drew you in. He let himself be drawn in and would never regret it.

He had healed quickly and married Claire the following summer. It turned out to be the social event of the year. The judge had presided over the ceremony, and not surprising anyone, Mary was Claire's matron of honor. Cletus gave up trying to talk Dan out of having him as his best man. Can you imagine anyone talking a car salesman out of a deal?

Mary and Cletus had quietly married during the winter after the fall storm. Ian had wanted Mary to have the big wedding that Kate, her mother, would have also wanted. But Mary would have none of that. She just wanted Cletus. Claire and Dan were witnesses when they were married by Judge Osborn, Claire's father. Ian couldn't have been happier for Mary. The wedding party had an intimate reception at Johnnie's restaurant in Jasper.

In the fall of that year, just before the elections, mayor Haskell announced that he wouldn't run for another term. He felt it was time for someone else to take over. He had served for three terms and thought he had a perfect replacement in mind – Claire Steele.

Claire was flattered but thought someone else should run for the election. Dan wouldn't hear of it. He knew she'd be perfect for the job. As did everyone else in Jasper. She ran unopposed. The election turnout was still high. She wanted everyone to express themselves at the polls. The community responded; they were thankful for her role at the Chamber of Commerce in helping with the planning for the new interstate highway spur that was being built. She was instrumental in guiding the community through the three years since she'd taken office.

She didn't know if she would run for reelection next year, there always seemed to be so much to get done. How would she find time to mount a campaign?

One event she was thinking about, was the rededication of the statue to the town's Civil War hero. It had been fifty years since the statue had been erected. This would be the one-hundred-year anniversary of the biggest battle he'd fought in – Gettysburg.

She had convinced the people on the planning committee to include a small ceremony at the statue as a part of the 4th of July celebration. The ceremony would include reading some of the material that had been placed in a time capsule when the monument was constructed and adding new material before the time capsule was resealed and placed back in the monument before it too was resealed. They were already planning on using items from a competition that the school was having in all the history classes. Being in the midst of the centennial of the Civil War, this was an opportunity to focus on the local effects of the conflict.

It was only April, but Claire thought she should start things moving at the monument. She suspected that unsealing the monument and removing the time capsule from the vault would not be an easy task. She had met with a local supplier of funereal products and found out that a mason should be called in to consult with about unlocking the tomb at the monument. She had contacted a local mason, Phil Jackson, who was on his way to meet her at the monument this morning to discuss opening the tomb, if it were possible.

After Dan and Claire had married, they continued living in Claire's apartment for several years. However, when Mrs. Delancey had un-expectantly died last year, Dan had jumped at the chance of purchasing her boarding house. There had not been any long-term residents, just overnight guests, so Dan closed that business. Now it was their home. Dan loved the feel of the town. Each morning he would have his coffee out on the veranda facing the square before leaving for the course. Today he had held back, knowing that Claire would be out on the square with Phil at the monument. Dan was sitting there with his coffee while Claire and Phil were talking at the monument.

Phil had brought the implements he'd need to move the cover of the vault. He'd done this before, so it wasn't going to be difficult.

As she approached, he said, "Good morning Claire."

Claire was cheery, "Good morning Phil, what a beautiful spring morning."

He said, "That it is. Do you have the paperwork from the next of kin?"

Claire said, "Here it is, all filled out."

Phil said, "Good, I don't want any problems with the authorities." He said with a chuckle.

Claire said, "I can't believe this won't take long."

Phil had started setting up the tripod for the lift over the vault cover. "Well Claire, it's pretty basic technology – just heavy. That's how it all works. This granite vault is old school. Most vaults nowadays are concrete."

He brought in lifting clamps around the side edges of the cover and added stretcher bars, so the clamps wouldn't slip and damage the cover. He then fastened the four chains from the lifting eye to each of the clamps. When they were securely hooked in place, he began ratcheting the winch suspended beneath the tripod. After a few moments, as the tripod settled down hard against the ground, the cover began lifting from the vault.

Dan had been watching from the veranda and now that this was starting to happen, he had come over and stood beside Claire.

Claire said to him quietly, "Thanks."

Dan just nodded, watching the cover slowly rise. When it was about six inches above the vault, Phil pivoted it away from the vault and carefully lowered it onto several timbers he had placed adjacent to the vault.

The three of them looked down onto the casket.

Claire gasped.

Where was the time capsule?

April 19, 1861

News of the war came quickly to Jasper. The talk of the southern states leaving the union had dominated the conversations taking place around the dinner tables in Jasper during the winter months. With the return of spring, everybody's spirits had lifted a little – then plunged when word of what happened at Fort Sumter came through on the telegraph.

Jedidiah Prescott enlisted at once. This was his chance to escape. He was being given a party before he left, but most on Sycamore Hill seemed relieved that he would be gone. Ruth would miss him, maybe a little. Perhaps if they'd been able to have a child, things would have been different, maybe not.

Henry and Sarah had gotten to really know each other. They were careful when around Ezekiel, to be sure, but they were closer. Ezekiel could see it too. He hadn't said anything. He didn't have to; they could see it in his face from time to time.

Henry wasn't sure how much longer he could stay. He hadn't said anything to anyone but Jack – maybe they should go now.

Ezekiel and his wife were hosting the party for Jedidiah to send him off. Most of the nearby neighbors had come to the farm to see Jedidiah, wish him well, tell him to stay safe. After all, he was going off to fight for them, wasn't he? An ambrotypist had come up to the house and captured a picture of Ruth and Jedidiah as well as several others that could afford his fee. He had written down specifics about how to color the images after they were developed. The coloring was a separate fee that would double the cost – if the customer asked for it. The blue eyes of both Ruth and Jedidiah would dominate the other muted colors of the ambrotype.

The evening of the party was unusually warm for late April. Everyone had finished eating and had broken up into groups discussing the war. Nothing much had really happened yet, but the older men knew better – soon it would start in earnest. Several had fought in Mexico. They knew the optimism wouldn't last.

Sarah pulled Henry aside and asked him to walk with her – away from all this talk of war. They moved away from the house, out towards the pond. She wanted to get far enough away so she didn't have to listen to the boasting – the false bravado of those yet to leave for the war, if they ever did.

Henry had been silent. He wasn't prone to take part in these discussions. He knew Ezekiel would dominate the conversation for some time and welcomed the chance to avoid it - for even a short time - with Sarah.

As they made their way to the far side of the pond, Sarah led him to the large sycamore at the outlet of the pond. The ground here wasn't as damp as nearer the water. She sat down on the ground and told Henry to sit beside her.

"Come on down here Henry. You're towering over me almost as badly as the sycamore."

Henry smiled, "Sorry, I was just looking out over the water. It's beautiful here, isn't it?"

Sarah said, "It truly is, that's why I wanted you to come out here with me and share this." As she waved her arm out indicating the expanse of the pond and beyond to the woods and farmhouse.

As Henry sat, she sidled up closer to him. Henry looked at her – she was so beautiful. So was Ruth, although she always seemed more distant to Henry. Sarah was more outgoing and had a warmth about her ... Henry was falling in love with Sarah.

Sarah knew this. She also knew Henry would probably leave. She could see the turmoil in him. As much as he tried to honor Ezekiel – he had to fight his true feelings and wouldn't be able to hide them much longer.

The two sat there for some time – both lost in their thoughts ... Henry reached down to Sarah's face and turned it gently, so he could kiss her.

As he was beginning to pull his lips from hers, she pulled him back to her.

After a long kiss, she stood up. She reached out to him to get him up to his feet - she led him deeper into the woods, away from the pond, away from everyone ...

~ *April 20, 1861* ~

Dear Diary, Henry's gone. I thought he would have left before now. As much as I think I love him, I couldn't tell him. He's usually so quiet, I wish I'd told him. I may never know how he may have truly felt about me ...the war and all.

His last words were to ask me to look after Jack while he was gone. Jack stands in the corner of the paddock at night, looking across to the pond and the sycamore by the path that leads into the woods and down to the mill.

The sycamores are all in full bloom now. Soon the planting will begin. I'll miss seeing Henry with Jack out in the fields like last spring.

~ 8 ~

That morning, Cletus, Mary and Chip were having breakfast in MacGregor's. It had only been a week since Mary found out about the move into the farmhouse. Chip had discussed this earlier with Dan and knew there was some work required before the Armstrong family could move into the farmhouse. It was agreed that Chip would head up the move and help with putting the house back in order. Cletus began working up there when he could, but the golf season was just starting to really pick up, so his time was limited.

Chip was great. He and Mary were picking out the paint schemes, the move needed to start soon or the remodeling in the mill would fall behind schedule. They had already decided that a new furnace was needed, it had been ordered, and it would be delivered later in the week. They were going to move all the appliances from the apartment, since the apartment was next on Chips' construction timetable. Her apartment, and the rest of the second floor of the stone mill building, was going to become MacGregor's restaurant. The third floor, above the apartment, was going to be thoroughly cleaned and used for storage space. The kitchen would be in the adjacent, "newer", section of the clubhouse which now contained all the office space. The new kitchen would be double the size of the old one.

All this work could now begin as soon as the apartment was vacated. Chip could start work on this immediately. The plan was to work through the summer on the restaurant and pub and move into them in the late fall, or winter, after golf. During the next winter, Chip would begin work on the golf course offices and expanded locker rooms. This work would be ongoing after the golf season started but couldn't be avoided. At least it didn't involve a lot of duplicate moving. They'd make do until everything was accomplished. The plan right now stretched out to just over two years.

Chip had also proposed a major renovation of the exterior of the clubhouse. He and Phil had come up with the idea of refacing the newer sections to more closely resemble the 'Mill' portion of the clubhouse. Everyone was excited about this, but it would have to wait until everything else was taken care of.

The morning rush of golfers had dwindled, the restaurant was empty of customers. Ian had been in and out of the conversation about the move into the farmhouse. He was glad that Mary and Cletus would have their own space away from the course. He looked up as Dan and Claire came into the room. They were closely followed by Phil Jackson and none of them looked very happy.

As the three of them approached the table where Cletus, Mary and Chip were talking, Ian came out and joined them. He said, "Claire, are you all right?"

Claire nodded her head and sat down beside Mary. As Phil sat down next to Chip, Dan quietly said, "We need to keep this quiet, just amongst ourselves, but we've got a big problem."

Ian sat down next to Claire while Dan leaned down on the table and said, "Phil just opened the vault."

Claire had tears coming down her cheeks, "The time capsule wasn't there."

Ian was next, "Phil how could this happen? When did this happen? Do you have any idea?"

Phil looked around, "None. I don't think that cover has ever been disturbed. There are no marks on it, anywhere. Everything looks untouched."

Claire said, "Why would anybody do such a thing? Why? What would they gain? As far as I know from what I've read, the time capsule was the only object in there. It was just a collection of printed material about the past and maybe some predictions about the future. The same sort of stuff you read about in other capsules. Nothing of any value."

Dan tried to calm her down. "Claire, we'll get to the bottom of this, there has to be an explanation." Dan looked up at everyone. "That's why we came up here. We'll need help figuring this out. We don't want this public knowledge. We don't know when this happened, but this is serious. This kind of thing just doesn't happen in Jasper."

Claire said, "This would kill daddy if he finds out."

Everybody nodded in agreement. The Judges' health was beginning to slip a little. He was rarely out on the course now. He would come up to talk to Ian and others at the course but couldn't play a full 18 holes of golf any longer. He just enjoyed being with his friends at the course.

Cletus had yet to say anything, which was his way. His friends around the table were used to this. He usually reserved his comments, but when he made them, they listened. He said, "Claire, I don't mean to pry into anything, but how much do you know about your Great-Grandfather? It seems that if we can't mention any of this just yet to the Judge, you're our only source of information about him."

Mary could see where his was headed, and she agreed. "Claire, Cletus is right. We've got to learn some more about your Great-Grandfather. Maybe we can find out who would want to cause something like this to happen. Maybe somebody with a grudge against the family."

Dan didn't want anybody really pressing Claire on this, but he had to agree that this might help. "Claire, think this over, we don't need to rush into this. I don't want you upset. Why don't we give it a day or two? We'll make sense out of this."

Claire had calmed down a little. "Give me a little time. There're some papers at home that dad has given me. Things he doesn't want to see lost or thrown out. He's been going through things at his house recently, I've tried to keep him from doing it, but he seems a little obsessed at times with making sure I have things of his that he thinks are important. I should mention to all of you though, that Henry Hawkins is not really my Great-Grandfather. Henry married my great-grandmother after her first husband, my real Great-Grandfather, died. We just grew up thinking of Henry as our Great-Grandfather. Dad was named after him, it's just easier to let everybody call him my Great-Grandfather." You could see that it still upset her, even if Henry wasn't her actual Great-Grandfather."

Dan stood up, "Come on Claire, I'm taking you home."

Claire quietly got up and left with Dan. The others remained at the table.

When they'd left, Ian asked Phil, "You're sure the vault hadn't been tampered with?"

Phil responded, "I'm almost positive. I looked that cover over closely before I hooked onto it. That's a polished granite cover that looks like it was put on yesterday. I don't know how anybody could have touched it. Especially right out in the middle of the square like it is. Any rig other than what I use would have left some marks. Somebody would have seen or heard something, look where it is."

~ 9 ~

The next several days passed quickly. Dan had convinced Claire that everything could be handled. If they couldn't sort out the problems, they would just present what they knew to the town. Everyone would understand, he told her. The town hero may have been her Great-Grandfather, but he belonged to the townspeople as well. From all he'd been told by everyone, Henry Hawkins came back from the war, not just a survivor, but someone who had stood tall and saved lives by his actions.

The town would stand behind the Judge and Claire. Maybe someone would be able to shed some light on all this. There weren't many townspeople left that would remember the ceremony in 1888, they would have been young children. But maybe there was something from the 1913 ceremony that people remembered that would help. Anyway, that could wait for the time being. Right now, they had to keep quietly investigating.

Dan and Chip were starting their day with a quick construction progress report while having a coffee in MacGregor's. Ian was headed over to join them this morning, Chip wanted to share something he'd found last night with Ian.

Ian sat down as Chip pulled a large book out of his briefcase that he used to carry his paperwork in while away from his office. He sat this down in front of Ian and opened it to a page he'd marked with a small slip of paper halfway through the book.

He said, "Ian, I thought you might be interested in this. I found it buried in a bottom drawer of the desk in the mill office. It's a ledger from the mill from around 1870. I remember you talking about your father-in-law, Tavis McDonald. There's an entry here where the owner of the mill, a Josiah Mueller, is paying Tavis McDonald seven dollars and fifteen cents in wages for a week's work."

Ian squinted down at the text. "Well I'll be." Said Ian. "Josiah was Kates' grandfather. He owned the mill. When Kates' mother Mary married Tavis he was working at the mill. Later they took over the farm up on the hill. Josiah left the farm to Mary when he died. Mary's mother had already died. I think her name was Sarah. Josiah had gotten rid of the mill by then. That was sometime in the 1900's."

He continued flipping through the book, seeing names of people that had done business at the mill. Seeing the accounts of the supplies that Josiah had purchased to keep the mill running. Really a history of the farming that took place around Jasper before the turn of the century.

Ian continued, "I always liked Tavis. He was from Scotland too. That's how I met Kate. Tavis and Mary had come across for a visit and brought Kate. They stayed all summer. I probably had something to do with delaying their departure. Once I met Kate, I never wanted to let go of her."

Chip and Dan had been quiet, listening to Ian.

Chip finally said, "Well Ian, you should keep that book. I'm surprised it's survived down there without getting damaged."

Ian said, "Thank you Chip, I'm glad you found it."

Chip said, "Well I'll probably come across more things that should stay in the family. I won't throw any items out until you've looked everything over."

Dan asked Chip, "So you're making progress down there then?"

Chip said, "It's slow but, I keep working at it. I think most of the machine shop stuff could be moved out now. You should take a look at it with Ian and see what you think. I assume you don't want to keep any of it to use here. It's pretty much an antique collection. Maybe you could donate it to a museum or something like that."

Dan agreed, "Ian we should get down there and take a look at this stuff when you get a chance, okay?"

Ian agreed, "Sure, maybe a little later today. We'll see how busy it gets in here. Bruce will be with me later. I can probably get away long enough to see what's down there."

"Great", said Chip, "That'll help. The sooner I can move some stuff out of there, the sooner I'll be able to give you an idea of how the pub could look. I think it's going to be nice – with all the stonework and beams. I think we need more light in there though. We should have Phil make a quick inspection and see if we can add a couple windows in the walls without causing any structural problems. I'd be great if we had more windows looking out at the pond."

Dan jumped in, "Cletus told me he's going to have some more cherry for you to work with. He came across another recent windfall up there on the hill. He's stockpiling some of the better-looking trunks for you. When you get around to the cabinetry, you'll have no shortage of material."

Chip stood up, "Well, you've got me excited. I'm off to do some painting with Mary. We're going to be installing the furnace up there today. Once the painting is finished in a couple days, they can move."

Ian was quiet, but after a moment added, "I know I'll miss having everybody so close after they're gone, but this is for the best. They have to have lives of their own. They're going to love it up on the hill."

Dan stood also, "Well, I've got to get going, lots to do today. Ian, come get me when you're ready to look at the stuff down there if you need my help."

With that, they headed off to start their workday.

~ 10 ~

Claire knew that sooner or later she'd have to tell her father about what had happened at the monument. The Judge may have slowed down a bit, but she knew he'd find out about what had happened before much longer. She wanted to be the one who told him, and she had decided she couldn't wait any longer. Besides, he might be able to help. She just didn't want to see him hurt.

He rarely went to his office in the courthouse anymore. He was more comfortable at home. He had a small office that he puttered around in. She knew he missed the routine of the court, the academic side of things, the legal investigating – the writing.

She let herself into his house and called out for him. "Dad are you here?"

He answered, "I'm in here Claire. Come on in."

She proceeded through into his office. "You're in here? I thought maybe you'd be outside, it's so nice outside – I think summer's not too far off. You should enjoy the spring flowers while you can. They'll be gone once it heats up."

He said, "You're right, I should get out. I just wanted to finish some things in here. What are you up to today?"

Claire sat, "I just wanted to talk."

The judge said, "Oh, oh", he said chuckling, "This can't be good. The mayor pays a surprise visit to me, before going to work!"

Claire said, "Dad, really, I just wanted to say hi. But I do want to talk to you for a minute. Okay?"

The judge tried to stop smiling, but couldn't completely wipe it from his face, "Okay Claire, what's on your mind?"

Claire was a little frustrated with him but continued, "Dad, you know we're going to open the vault and retrieve the time capsule for the ceremony in July, right?"

The judge's smile was gone, his demeanor sobered. "So soon, It's always seemed farther off."

Claire said, "Dad. I had the vault opened yesterday. It was just Dan and Phil Jackson, the mason that was recommended that I use to open the vault."

The judge was listening closely.

Dad, "I don't know how to say this without hurting you, but ..." she just didn't know how to continue.

The judge looked at her, "It wasn't there was it?"

Claire looked at her father dumbfounded. "How did you know, who told you. I asked that everything be kept quiet about it until I could talk with you. Did Dan already speak to you?"

The judge smiled, "Calm down Claire, nobody said anything to me, your secret's safe"

She looked at him.

He said, "I've always known. I'm the last one to see everything before the vault was closed up."

May 27, 1861

In Jasper, they received word that Jedidiah had died of dysentery while encamped at Wheeling, Virginia. The army was preparing to move out against the rebels the next day in what would become the first land-based engagement of the Civil War. During the war, most casualties amongst the soldiers were from sickness, not battlefield injuries.

This was the first death of any of those that had left Jasper for the war. The community was shocked but, by and large, didn't really know how to behave about his death. Everyone expressed their condolences to Ruth, they truly felt sorry for her. But most everyone in Jasper didn't know Jedidiah very well. He was an outsider and hadn't shown any particular interest in community activities.

In the parlor of the Jennings home, Jedidiah's ambrotype that he had given Ruth when he left, was draped in black lace. A stoic reminder of her husband.

Henry hadn't been heard from at all. Although he had only been in Jasper a short time, he had made friends, and to a large extent, he had considered Jasper his home. Much of his contact with others was by way of the mill. Although the mill was only about two miles outside of Jasper, most of the farmers living out in that direction tended to congregate at the mill, rather than traveling the extra distance into Jasper, except for something special that could only be found in Jasper.

Isaac Mueller was getting older and let Josiah handle most of the heavy work around the mill. He had others that worked for him during the fall harvest season when the mill was busiest. During the rest of the year the mill was a combination store, blacksmith shop, restaurant and public house. Isaac was licensed to sell liquor and also 'acted' as a postmaster for the small office set up in the basement. This saved a lot of extra traveling and seemed to sit well with the postmaster in Jasper. The fact that Isaac had access to the mail was why no one had heard from Henry. It was also why Henry had not heard from Sarah.

Ezekiel had met with Isaac not long after Henry had left. He convinced Isaac to intercept the mail to and from Henry. Ezekiel wanted to do everything he could to prevent any further involvement of Henry with Sarah. He figured he could grind Sarah down and convince her that marrying Josiah was in her best interest, but only if Henry was out of the picture. The way he looked at it, Henry was probably going to get killed anyway, why complicate Sarah's life?

For his part, Isaac felt the same. A marriage between Josiah and Sarah would benefit everyone. Ezekiel's farm had become one of the largest around. The combination of the farm and the mill concentrated in the glen as a joint family business would secure their fortunes far into the future.

So far, their scheme was working. Any doubts Isaac had about tampering with the mail had vanished. It had been weeks since any mail had come through from Henry. Ezekiel was probably right. Henry may have already died, just like Jedidiah.

~ June 5, 1861 ~

I've written to Henry again. No one has heard from him.

There's so much I wish I'd said to him before he left. We've heard that some of the other's that left for the war have died. One of Mr. Bartlett's sons, Michael, was killed at Fairfax Courthouse in Virginia.

~ 11 ~

Mary and Cletus were up at the farmhouse. Mary had driven up with Katie by way of the road that wrapped around the far side of the hill. Cletus had driven straight up the hill in his cart. He could now come up through the glen without too much trouble since he'd quickly cut a pathway through the woods near the pond. He'd need to do a lot more work to make it truly usable by Mary in a cart, but for now, he could get through and help with the move as his schedule permitted. Chip was basically handling everything. The quicker they moved; the quicker Chip could start on some serious renovation work in their apartment to turn it into the new restaurant.

The mustiness of the farmhouse was almost gone. They had repainted several of the rooms and would finish the rest this week. The furnace would be delivered sometime this morning, Cletus just wanted to make a final check of the basement to make sure it could be moved in without any issues. Ian and Kate had continued using a wood fired furnace that required quite a bit of attention in the winter. It was being replaced by a coal fired furnace that wouldn't require quite as much maintenance.

Cletus had hired one of the boys that was mowing at the course, to work around the farmhouse to clean up the yard and try and make the grounds presentable. It would take a year or two for a yard to get reestablished, but it already looked a lot better after the years of neglect since Ian and Mary had left.

Dan had been a little vague about how much of the property in the vicinity of the farmhouse that they'd be responsible for maintaining. For now, though, Cletus just wanted to be able to see across to the pond and be able to keep an eye on Katie when she was outside. He didn't think Katie would play in the water, she was warned often enough and seemed to understand how dangerous it might be if she fell into the water. They needed to get her started on swimming lessons this summer.

When he entered the farmhouse, he found Mary and Chip hard at work in the kitchen applying a second coat of light-yellow paint. Well, some of it was making it onto the walls, a good share of it seemed to be on Mary.

Cletus couldn't help himself, "Morning Chip. Looks like you'll have just about enough yellow to finish this up, you cut it close though."

Mary was waiting for it, "I know, I know. Not everyone is as neat as you when it comes to painting. I'm a little rusty, but I'm getting better. If you think you can do better, here's the brush."

Cletus said to Chip, "Like I said Chip, excellent job!"

Chip was chuckling, he'd seen this show play out several times before. He liked being with Cletus and Mary at times like this. They were just fun to be around.

Mary ignored the comment and continued to smooth out a brush full of paint she'd applied just before Cletus entered.

Chip said to Cletus, "You didn't have to come all the way up here. We're all set downstairs for the furnace; they should be here anytime with it."

Cletus responded, "Well, I just wanted to make sure you didn't need any more help up here for it when they came."

Chip answered, "Really, we're fine. In fact, they said they'll have three men here to unload everything and get it down into the basement, so you don't need to stick around."

Cletus said, "Well if you're sure you don't need the extra help, I'll get out of your way here and get back to the course."

Mary had finished with the paint she was working with and said, "Chip you can take off too. You don't have to stay until the furnace arrives. This is just about finished; I can do the rest. I'm sure you have other things you'd like to do besides watching me spill paint all over the place."

Chip said, "If you're set here for a while, I'd like to get back also, there's a couple other things I wanted to get done today."

Mary said, "It's okay, I'm almost done. Once the furnace arrives, I'm going back down also. I've got to get some lunch for Katie and see how Susan's handling things in the restaurant."

Chip began cleaning up and sealing his paint can. He had turpentine in the barn and left to clean his brush.

Cletus said to Mary, "Mary it looks great in here, everything does."

Mary said to him, "I know, everything's so bright and cheery. There's so much more light coming into these rooms than the apartment. And you know what else?"

Cletus shook his head.

Mary said, "Listen"

Cletus listened.

Mary said, "Do you hear that?"

Cletus shook his head again, looking a little puzzled. He said to her, "I don't hear anything"

"Exactly!" was all Mary said.

Cletus smiled, she was right, "I guess I've gotten used to the noises around the course. You're right, this is nice."

He came over to her and carefully kissed her, trying not to get any paint on himself or touching anything that was still wet.

He said, "I'll leave you to your artistic endeavors. Chip's probably ready out there."

As Mary looked out the door after Cletus, she spotted Katie coming back from the garage where she had been exploring.

Chip joined Cletus and off they went towards the pond in Cletus' cart.

~ 12 ~

When they got back to the clubhouse, Chip asked Cletus if he had a couple minutes to join him in his basement office. Cletus said 'sure' and followed him in through the door that Chip had added that let out onto the clubhouse patio.

Chip said to him, "What I wanted you to look at are these mill wheels over here.

Chip led Cletus into the far corner of the shop. This section was firmly based on the ground, not cantilevered out over the stream like the other half of the room. The floor consisted of stone slabs that had been neatly jointed to provide a smooth surfaced workroom that heavy machinery could be set down on. Stacked against the wall, lying flat on the stone floor were several sets of mill stones. Some had obviously been well used, others looked almost brand new.

Most were about the same diameter, about four feet. At the bottom of a pile of same size wheels were a pair of stones that appeared to be bigger, perhaps five feet or more in diameter. Chip pointed to these bigger stones which appeared to be new, never used.

Chip said, "Here's what I wanted you to see. Those two stones on the bottom have to be unused. Look at the others."

Cletus looked at the other stones. He agreed. "You're right Chip, those are like brand new."

Chip continued, "What I was wondering, is if we could use these as a part of the decor in either the pub down here, or the restaurant, upstairs?"

Cletus thought this over. "We should show these to Ian and Mary. I think they'd look great in both places, but I know they've had a lot of ideas about what the pub and the restaurant should look like. They are impressive, aren't they?"

Chip agreed, "They're just so massive. Especially those two on the bottom. They're new, I'm sure they'd look good someplace inside. Although I'm not even sure how I'm going to move them."

Cletus looked around, curious about the room. "You're right, I wonder how they were moved and stacked like they are?"

Chip had spent some time looking over the heavy equipment. "Well they had some sort of block and tackle arrangement that could be set up in different parts of the room. I've seen some spots in the beams where it could have been attached. They probably also used a tripod type arrangement on the stones that could be set up anywhere on the floor. If you look at the edge of the wheels, you'll see two pockets on them that must have allowed a grappling arrangement to hook into the stones. Then the winch could hook onto the grapple. The stones could be pivoted using the grapple to set them down on their edge and be moved by carefully rolling them."

Cletus was examining the overhead beams and spotted the holes that Chip was referring to.

Chip continued, "I've been reading a little about the milling process and they had to swap out stones pretty frequently because of the wear and tear on the stones. They'd change the stones when the milling furrows wore out and have a stone dresser or mason recut the furrows while the stones were out of service. It must have really been something to see a mill like this in operation."

Cletus was still wandering around looking at the beams and the floor of the apartment overhead. He stopped at an area that had been more recently 'filled in' with newer lumber.

Chip pointed upwards, "That's where the stones were mounted. The lower stone, the bedstone, was fixed in place in the hole. The upper stone, the runner stone, sat above it and rotated nearly against it causing the grinding action to break down the grain."

Cletus said, "So all they did when the stones were removed was to fill in the hole, so the floor above would be smooth?"

Chip agreed, "Yeah, that's what it looks like. See the big beams on either side of the hole. There're holes in them that probably had large angle irons bolted in place. The pictures I've looked at, show these leveling bolts mounted to angles reaching upwards so that the bedstone could be accurately held up close the running stone. The miller upstairs had a lever that very precisely held the desired gap between the stones depending on what was being milled. He could lower the running stone to just the right gap for whatever type of grain he was working with. The bedstones are actually a little bit convex and the running stones are slightly concave, so the grinding action actually forces the material out away from the center of the stones."

Cletus looked at the massive beams on either side of the hole. They would have had to hold the entire weight of the bedstone. There was no other support for the stone. He looked at the hole – something wasn't quite right.

"Look at the beam on the left side of the opening. It looks newer than the one on the right. The left one was sawn and doesn't have any through holes in it. The right one looks to have been hand hewn."

Chip said, "If you go upstairs, you'll see that the beams above this are placed to support the drive mechanism that engaged on the stones. There're also some holes in the beams up there, like down here, to accommodate the block and tackle to lower the stones down thru the hole to the floor. Look at the floor right here. See where the stones marked up the floor when they were lowered?"

Cletus looked down studying the floor and agreed. Finally, he said, "Well, I've got to get back out there. When I see Mary, I'll tell her to take a look at these stones, they're impressive aren't they?" he said, as he waved at the stack back in the corner.

Cletus stared up at where the opening for the stones had been filled in, he shook his head and turned to leave.

Chip said, "Thanks for stopping, I'll have Ian take a look too."

Chip walked back to the pile of stones and stared at the two larger stones on the bottom of the pile.

~ 13 ~

Phil Jackson was really bothered by the missing time capsule. He somehow felt responsible, since he was the one who opened the vault. He was sure no one had tampered with the cover. He'd been back to the monument several times to reexamine the cover. It just didn't seem possible. As he puzzled over this mystery, another thought came to mind, and this was more serious. Finally, he made his mind up, he called Dan.

Dan was in his office when he got the call from Phil.

"Dan, Phil Jackson here."

Dan answered, "Phil, what's up, what can I do for you?"

Phil responded, "Dan, I've been giving this 'mystery' a lot of thought. Actually, it's all I've been thinking of. Can you meet me at the monument this morning? There's something I'd like to discuss with you privately."

Dan thought for a moment, "Sure Phil, I've got a little time this morning. I can't stay long, but why don't I drive down now, and meet you there. Is that okay?"

Phil said, "That would be great. I won't take up a lot of your time. I'll be there when you arrive."

Dan said goodbye and hung up. He walked out through to Curtis' office to let him know where he'd be.

"Curtis, I'm going into town on a quick errand. I won't be long. Anything you need from me for a while?"

Curtis responded, "Everything's under control here, take your time."

With that, Dan was off to Jasper. He jumped into his bright red Chevy pickup that seemed to be his vehicle of choice now. He still had a convertible in the garage but preferred the pickup which allowed him to haul around 'stuff' more conveniently. He made his way down the hill and into Jasper driving around behind the courthouse approaching the town square on a side street. As he passed the courthouse, he saw Claire's Corvette parked in its usual space behind the courthouse. She must be running errands this morning, or the car would have been left in their garage since she only had about a two-minute walking commute from their house across the square to the courthouse, where her office was.

Dan pulled up behind Phil's vehicle and parked. Phil was already over at the monument standing by the vault. He looked up from the vault cover when Dan approached.

"Morning Dan. Thanks for coming over."

Dan was glad to see Phil, "Good morning Phil. I appreciate you staying on top of this situation", said Dan nodding down toward the cover. "What's up?"

Phil carefully said, "Dan, I've been trying to figure out what happened here. Just like the rest of you. But there's something else I think we should do."

Dan said, "Sure, go ahead what's on your mind."

Phil continued, "Well Dan, I got a pretty good look at the casket while the vault was open. It's a steel model that was quite popular at the time. I'm not an expert on any of this, so maybe you'd like to call someone else in for this instead of me ..."

Dan calmed him, "Phil, you think we need to open the casket, don't you?"

Phil looked at Dan and nodded.

Dan said to him, "Thanks for calling me. This would be tough for Claire to handle."

Phil said to Dan, "Exactly. There're a couple reasons why I'd like to open the casket. First, these old caskets sometimes used a gasket to seal everything up – airtight. From what I've read, the contents can sometimes become liquefied."

Dan responded, "Really!"

Phil nodded, "Yeah, I don't want anyone to have to experience seeing that if the casket were opened."

Dan agreed, "You're right about that."

Phil said, "Secondly, sooner or later someone's going to suggest looking in there for the capsule. I'm curious. It's possible it got placed in there instead of simply laying it on top of the casket. I know Claire has read that, that's the way it was done. But it's possible ..."

Dan said, "Good thinking, I'm sure we need to open it just to be sure."

Phil said, "Well I have all the paperwork, the permission from the judge includes both the vault and the casket."

Dan said, "Yeah, you should quietly open the casket. Claire doesn't have to get involved at this stage. Then we'd know for sure."

Phil said, "Dan, I've got the equipment in my truck ..."

Dan said, "Then, let's do this right now."

~ 14 ~

Claire had left her father, after promising to not say anything to the others – yet. He asked her to keep the secret just a little longer, he had his reasons, he'd explain soon. He just asked for a day or two, that's all. Claire could see this was hard on her father, they both disliked secrets and neither had ever kept any from the other, or so she thought.

Claire's mother, Mildred, had died during the influenza pandemic in February of 1918. The surrounding community was not spared from this global disaster. Mildred had been a normal healthy adult which made her death all the more tragic. Claire was kept from her mother during the brief period of her illness and was spared. It seemed that most victims were middle aged adults that were otherwise quite healthy.

The result was that Claire was raised by her father with the help of a nanny until she was in her teens. The two shared everything, making this situation about the time capsule harder on Claire than she'd thought when she had looked into the vault.

As she sat in her office throughout the morning, all sorts of thoughts were flying through her head. What was going on? She had phoned Dan at the course, wanting to talk to him – she wouldn't keep any secrets from Dan. But she was told by Curtis that Dan had left the course to come into town. She thought he'd show up here before too much longer, so she sat and tried to focus on her work – without much success.

Phil had positioned his tripod over the vault and lifted the cover off to the side.

Dan stared down at the casket. It did look to be in remarkable condition for a steel casket.

Phil looked down at it, "That is some casket. I've only seen a couple other steel ones, but this one is in the best condition I've seen. That granite cover was some great fit for the vault."

Dan looked up at Phil.

Phil put a much smaller winch on the tripod than he'd used to raise the lid of the casket. This was the only tricky part of this business. Phil couldn't be sure exactly how the lid was fastened. He'd seen all manner of screws and locking mechanisms on caskets. Some also involved seals or gaskets, but that wasn't usually the case. Most times, air was allowed to enter the casket, so the remains slowly mummified.

He fed two straps beneath the casket, it was resting on small cross pieces built into the bottom of the vault. These allowed the ropes used to initially lower the casket into the vault, to be removed. He brought the straps up to his winch and slowly began lifting the casket from the vault. When it was above the top edge of the vault, he pivoted it to the side and laid the casket on the ground.

As he suspected, the lid lifted easily after he had removed a series of bolts around the periphery of the cover. The casket was a metal one which was quite typical in the late 1800's, especially just after the war when so many bodies were being buried. This burial had been in 1888, but had still used a steel casket, rather than the more decorative wooden models which were just becoming fashionable. Apparently, there was no sealing gasket involved with this casket.

As he lifted the lid clear of the casket and they swung it around clear of the vault, he was glad that he and Dan were handling this alone.

As he and Dan stared down into the open casket all they saw were several stones. No capsule. No body.

They looked at each, stunned.

Dan spoke first.

"Put the cover back on."

Phil nodded. they swung the cover back over the casket, reattached it to the casket and quickly lowered the casket down into the vault. There was no need for extreme neatness now.

Dan helped him switch the winches back around, so the vault cover could be handled. Slowly he lowered it back down against the edges of the vault. When he finished, he disassembled everything and loaded it back into his truck with Dan's help. The two hadn't spoken for several minutes.

Finally, Dan said, "Can you come back up to the club with me?

Phil silently nodded.

Dan walked back to his truck, climbed in and headed back up to the golf course followed by Phil.

September 5, 1862

Dewey Carson lay crouched behind a large stone. The stone had been laboriously moved towards the edge of the field by the farmer whose cornfield it now occupied. But the stone had been too big to lift into the stone wall, so it just sat there - as stones so often do – protecting Dewey. The ground sloped away from Dewey. A quarter of a mile away, the corn ended as the ground fell off into a stream that cut through the farmland. The corn was ready for harvesting, but with the fighting so close by, none of the fields in the area had been tended to in the last couple of months. The mid-afternoon sun was baking Dewey. He would have preferred to remain back in the woods but had moved up here when ordered to. He had to admit, he could see more of the field out here in front of the woods. He could look both east and west quite a distance, not that he saw anything worth noting. It was just a hot, late summer, afternoon. About the only sound he could hear was the constant buzz of the cicadas in the trees behind him.

The man lying beside him, looking out from behind the other side of the rock towards the creek wasn't so sure. On the far side of the creek there was movement. He carefully brought his rifle up. He laid it against the rock, pinning it there with his left hand. He squinted down the barrel, out across the field, down to the creek.

The slow methodical movement didn't startle Dewey, he had seen this play out more than a few times. Dewey brought his rifle up now also. He couldn't see anything, but he had to be ready. In situations like this, all hell tended to break loose without further warning. Dewey's breathing got a little quicker, a little shallower.

After several minutes, the man beside him slowly lowered his rifle. In a calm, quiet voice he said, "What'd I tell you about that? Take deeper breaths. Your tongue is probably against the roof of your mouth too, isn't it?"

Dewey lowered his rifle slowly. He whispered, "Sorry. What'd you see out there?"

Henry Hawkins rolled onto his back, now completely behind the stone and closer to Dewey. "Just a patrol, no officers. They're moving along the creek, not crossing it."

Dewey said to him, "I don't know how you can see that far without binoculars or a telescope. You sure about this?"

Henry looked at him. Dewey thought, 'Yup he's sure.'

The two of them laid there for another half an hour until Henry said, "Come on, let's head back. I want to report this, so they can send someone back out if this turns out to be something other than a routine patrol."

Quietly, the two of them crept back into the woods behind them before they stood. They picked their way through the trees quietly for several hundred yards before talking.

Dewey said to Henry, "That must have been five hundred yards to the creek. There's no way you could have hit anybody."

Henry turned to him. "You're not that far off with the distance. I was just like looking down the barrel. I might have hit him though."

Dewey scoffed. "You're good. I'll give you that. But five hundred yards - with a Sharps – without a scope?"

Henry said, "Some time we'll find out. Not today. No point in risking anything. All we were supposed to do was watch."

Dewey looked at him. "I know your orders. It's no secret. If you see a senior officer, you can take the shot."

Henry looked at him and smiled, "Not today. For a lot of reasons, it wasn't right."

They kept trudging deeper into the woods, heading away from the cornfield, back towards their camp. Henry looked at Dewey, he liked him. He had come into the regiment in the spring. He was a good shot. Henry told their Lieutenant he could make him a great shot. The Lieutenant went along with Henry. He told Dewey to stay close to Henry. The regiment had scouts, and they were good. They were good on their own, out in front, probing, looking for the enemy. They were all good shots. They handled themselves good on their own. They could all make good decisions and take independent action without jeopardizing the regiment. But they weren't like Henry.

Henry had shown up the previous summer. He was a replacement and had immediately impressed those that had seen him shoot. It wasn't that he was trying to impress anyone. He just had all the skills it took to be great. And he improved on them. In the several engagements he'd fought in, his skills didn't go unnoticed. He did all that was asked of him, and more. While he'd never had any formal military training, he soaked everything in. This was serious business, it wasn't some lark, like many of the kids seemed to think when they arrived. It didn't take long for these youngsters to realize it wasn't. In the year and a half Henry had been fighting, he'd aged ten years. He had quickly risen to the rank of sergeant and would probably go further if he wasn't killed first.

The Lieutenant had taken Dewey aside not long after being told to 'stay close' to Henry. He told Dewey that he knew he was good enough to be assigned to duty with the scouts, but he wanted someone to be with Henry on a regular basis. They had been sending Henry out beyond the other scouts. It was dangerous. He needed someone with him all the time. Someone he could rely on. The Lieutenant had used others. They got along with Henry, but Henry didn't want to get too close to anyone. The Lieutenant knew, as did most of the others, that

Henry had become more than just a good soldier. He had become an expert, cold blooded, assassin.

Henry and Dewey were close, but not in the sense that they were "friends". Henry could sense that Dewey was more than a good shot, but it took more than that at times to survive. Henry poured all of his knowledge that he could, into Dewey. He probably didn't understand all of it, yet. But he listened and watched. Dewey knew that Henry was something special, and it was his job to protect him while he learned from him.

~

Henry had an unending series of tidbits of knowledge to pass on to Dewey. That evening, around the campfire with the rest of the scouts, Henry watched Dewey drink his usual, second, large cup of coffee. Dewey could see Henry giving him that 'What are you doing now?' look, from across the fire.

Dewey looked back at Henry after finishing off the last of the coffee in his cup. Henry just sat there shaking his head. Dewey came over to Henry and sat down on the ground beside him. Henry looked at Dewey and skootched away from him, so they were several feet apart. Dewey bent his head down a little towards his chest and sniffed. "Do I stink that bad?" he said to Henry.

Henry laughed at him. "I won't comment on what you smell like. The other's here probably have an opinion though."

Everyone nearby chuckled. They all stank.

Henry said to him, "Turn towards me so we're directly opposite each other."

Dewey shuffled around in the dirt, so they were facing each other.

"Now" Henry said, "raise both arms, and point your index finger on each hand at me."

While everyone moved in closer to see what was happening, Dewey did as he was told.

Henry raised his arms and pointed his index fingers at Dewey's, they were about two inches from each other.

"Okay" Henry said, "close your eyes and count to sixty and keep pointing your fingers at mine, while I close my eyes too."

Dewey closed his eyes, as did Henry, and counted aloud to sixty. When he was done, and opened his eyes, his fingertips were nowhere near Henry's. Dewey looked around at the others. One of them said, "His never moved, Dewey."

Everyone was quiet now.

Henry said to Dewey, "I like a little coffee, but just a little. I usually water it down so there's only a hint of coffee flavor in it. I know you all think coffee gives you a little extra energy. It probably does. But that comes at a price. A high price for a marksman, maybe too high."

With that, Henry got up, moved back from the fire to walk to the scouts' supply wagon. He climbed in and rummaged around for a couple minutes and came out with a rifle. It was his Whitworth. He walked towards their tent, as Dewey was approaching. Dewey stopped when he saw the rifle. Henry saw that Dewey was staring at the rifle. It was no secret that Henry preferred the breech loading Sharps to the muzzle loading Whitworth. Henry said to Dewey, "I think we'll need the extra range." Just before entering the tent, Henry yelled back to the group at the campfire, "It keeps you up all night too!", and in a quieter voice said to Dewey, "Get some sleep Dewey, we may have a long walk ahead of us tomorrow if we can't find a couple of horses." With that, he went into his tent leaving everyone staring at their coffee cups.

Dewey hesitated, thinking a little time around the fire wouldn't hurt. But then he recalled the look on Henry's face and thought better of it. He entered their tent. Henry was looking the rifle over. As Dewey sat on the edge of his cot before laying down, he looked across at Henry. Henry looked up, his dark brown eyes met

Dewey's eyes - he was smiling as he said, "I think I know where Bobby Lee is going to be."

~ September 5, 1862 ~

Diary, Clarissa is growing so quickly. Josiah is such a good 'uncle' to her.

~ 16 ~

When Dan and Phil arrived at the course, it was after twelve. There was a lot of movement around the clubhouse. Some of the workers were in the process of getting their lunches in MacGregor's when Dan and Phil entered. They came up near the bar and waited for the crowd to thin out a little before they finally took a table in the back of the room. Ian was busy filling drink orders and there were some golfers that had decided to get a quick meal before finishing their round. Ian could see something was up. Dan and Phil were quiet, obviously waiting for things to quiet down. They'd glanced in his direction a couple times, as if they were trying to get his attention.

Susan had taken their order and they'd just been joined by Cletus before Ian had been able to walk over to their table.

Ian said, "You two look as though you wanted a word with me."

Dan glanced around and saw that it had slowed. Ian could take a couple minutes with them. Dan motioned for Ian to sit down.

He began, quietly he said, "We just opened the casket.", and he looked towards Phil.

Phil just slowly shook his head.

Ian said, "It wasn't in there either? I was hoping someone would think to look in there without me suggesting it."

Cletus was studying Phil.

Dan said, "We've got a bigger problem than the capsule."

They all looked at Dan as he said, "There wasn't anything in the casket. Nothing. Just a couple rocks."

Ian sat back, "Impossible!"

All Cletus could say was, "What's going on here?"

"I was going to ask the same question!" said Mary cheerily as she came up to the table.

They all looked at her. Their looks said it all.

She sat down next to Cletus, "What's happening?"

Cletus quietly said, "Phil and Dan opened the casket to check for the capsule – the casket's empty."

Mary turned to Dan and said, "You thought the capsule was in the casket?"

Dan nodded, "Phil thought the two of us should check before Claire got the idea to look on her own."

Mary looked at Phil, "Good thinking." was all she said.

She thought about this for a moment, no one else was adding anything as she looked around. "Where are we going to look next?"

Cletus looked at her, "Mary the casket was empty. Just some rocks in it. That's all."

Mary looked at Cletus, then it registered, and she looked back at Dan.

Dan said, "This just got a whole lot worse!"

Dan got up. Susan had just delivered the two meals. Nobody looked like they had any intention of eating, something was happening, so she excused herself and went back to the kitchen for other orders.

Dan said, "I've got to find Claire and talk to her. Tell Curtis I may not be back this afternoon." He left MacGregor's to talk to his wife, to try and make some sense of this with her. They'd have to also talk to the judge. He hoped the judge could handle this, it would be hard enough concerning the capsule, but his great-grandfather ...? How would he take all this in?

~ 17 ~

Dan found Claire in her office at the courthouse. She had settled down from earlier in the morning. The quiet time in her office had done her good. She was glad to see Dan when he popped his head inside her door.

"Hey darling, how about joining me for a late lunch?" he said as he came through the doorway.

Claire got up and came over to him, "This must be serious. Did you think you'd forgotten our anniversary or something?" she said smiling at him.

"Nope. Just thought you'd like a quiet meal at Johnnies."

She said to him, "That would be perfect. I didn't get anything accomplished here this morning."

As she collected her coat and purse, Dan said to her, "That doesn't surprise me. I know this whole thing with the capsule has really gotten to you."

They continued walking out towards their cars, Dan said, "Hey let's walk over there, Okay?"

Claire smiled, "Sure it's a gorgeous day, it'll feel good to walk a little. I drove over here after seeing dad this morning."

Dan continued to watch her as they came down the front steps of the courthouse. They crossed the street to walk through the square on their way to Johnnies. Their path took them right past the monument. They stopped to look at it as well as the vault. After several minutes Dan took her hand and guided her away from all this, continuing on toward Johnnies.

It was only three or four blocks away depending on how you counted the zig zag route around the square. When they came through the door, Nancy Pagano looked up and broke out into a smile at the sight of Dan. He frequented Johnnies as much as Teddy now. He'd become a close friend. She came around the counter to greet them.

"Claire, Dan, how nice to see you. Are you joining us for lunch or just something quick?"

Dan said to her, "Lunch please, Nancy dear, for me and my bride here." as he nodded towards Claire.

Claire leaned in close to Nancy and said, "What a flirt he is. Hi Nancy."

Nancy led them into the dining area and sat them in a booth. She had menus and placed them on the table.

Dan said to her, "How about a nice red wine – your choice, pick out something you think we'd like."

Nancy raised her eyebrows a little, looked at Claire, then swiveled around to go find some wine.

Claire said to Dan, "Alright, now I'm worried, you never drink wine."

Dan became serious. "Claire, we need to talk. I don't want to upset you any more than you already are but there's something you need to know about, over there", he said as he motioned back towards the square."

Claire nodded, "It's okay, I've calmed down a bit. I know we can work this out." She paused for a moment, "I discussed it this morning with dad."

Dan looked at her. He knew she wouldn't wait long. He hoped it had gone okay. "How did it go? Is he okay?"

Claire smiled a little, "He knew. He's always known."

Dan was shocked.

~ 18 ~

Dan felt they should talk to the judge immediately. He was sure the judge knew about the empty casket. Where was Henry Hawkins actually buried?

During their lunch, Dan could see that Claire had settled down about the capsule. When their meal was finished, Dan suggested they splurge and have one of Russel's cannoli. Dan said to Claire, "Why don't we split one?"

Claire agreed, "That would be perfect. I won't tell Mary that you're cheating. I know she's watching what you eat at MacGregor's. I get regular progress reports from her."

Dan said, "I suspected as much. I know her heart's in the right place, but I love cannoli."

When the cannolo came, Claire split it in half and slowly enjoyed the pastry.

Dan finished quickly and said to Claire, "So now that our problem is twice as big as it was, what do we do?"

Claire looked at him, "Let's give daddy the day or two he needs and let him explain about the capsule when he's ready."

Dan said, "Assuming there's a good explanation about the capsule, the ceremony at the monument should not be a problem. But what about the casket?"

Claire said, "What do you mean, 'what about the casket'?"

Dan said, "Well I know Henry's your dad's grandfather and all, but if he's not in the casket, where is he?"

Claire processed this for a second or two and dropped her fork.

Dan looked at her, "Claire I didn't mean to upset you, but …"

Claire drew a breath, "Dan what are you talking about?"

Dan said, "Claire, where is Henry? Is your dad a part of this as well as the capsule?"

Claire said, "He's not in the casket?"

Dan said, "Isn't that what you meant when you said your dad 'knew'?

Claire said, "He knew the time capsule wasn't in the vault on top of the casket where it was supposed to be. He said nothing about the casket. I didn't ask."

Dan explained that earlier he and Phil had gone back to the monument and reopened the vault to look in the casket.

Claire got up, "Come on, let's find out what's going on here?"

Dan stopped at the front counter to pay the bill and hurriedly made an excuse to Nancy that they had to leave. He thanked her for the delicious meal and rushed out to catch up with Claire.

~ 19 ~

The judge was sitting at his kitchen table finishing a sandwich when Claire and Dan came up onto the rear porch. Claire knocked lightly on the door and let herself in.

The judge said to her, "Claire, twice in one day. I'm flattered." Then he saw Dan behind her.

Claire sat down at the table, opposite the judge. Dan sat at the table between them.

"Dad what's going on out there? Claire said as she waved her hand off towards the square.

The judge responded, "Claire, I said I'd explain. I just need to find the right way. That's why I asked for a day or two."

Dan thought he should step in here, "Dad, we appreciate this may be hard for you. You can tell us, we'll understand."

The judge turned to Dan and smiled, "You know son, I believe you. And you too Claire. I'm trying to understand this myself. It was a long time ago; I was a young man. The request was a little odd, but your grandmother was really something. I swear she could get anybody to do anything. She's the one who held the whole family together."

Claire had relaxed a little. She put her hand on Dan's.

Dan said, "Go ahead dad."

The judge said, "Well, she came to me before the ceremony and said we couldn't put the capsule in there on the casket. I asked her, 'What do you mean?'. She looked at me in a way I'd never seen before and said, 'Henry, please trust me on this. Don't put the capsule in the vault. I have my reasons. Perhaps I'll explain them to you in the future, but for now – please help me, trust me.'"

Claire said, "I don't understand. What did grandma give as her explanation when she finally told you?"

The judge said, "That's the problem Claire, she never explained it. It wasn't long after that when I went off to law school and then after that to fight in the war. She never told me."

Dan looked at the judge, understanding now what was bothering the judge. 'Not knowing'. The judge's life was built on truth and justice, not secrecy.

The judge continued, "All these years ... Eventually I put it in the back of my mind. I rationalized that either nothing would come of 'opening' the capsule. Or that I'd be gone before it was opened. That was wrong of me – to leave you this mess. Claire, I'm sorry."

Claire understood also. She looked at her father, visibly older now. She said, "Dad, I understand. You should have said something before ..."

"Claire, I tried. You don't know how many times I thought about saying something. It just never seemed like the time or place to bright it up. But now – I'm glad you know."

The judge got up from the table. He said, "Give me a minute here." He left the kitchen and returned moments later. He sat back down at the table.

He said to Claire, "Here's a key", handing a key to Claire. "It's to a safety deposit box. Clarissa put the capsule in there fifty years ago. It's never been opened, by me or anybody else."

Claire stared at the key. She said to him, "How did you ..."

The judge chuckled, "Oh it wasn't as difficult as you'd imagine. I remember it like it was yesterday. The weather that day was nasty. Nothing seemed to go according to plan during the ceremony. It was pouring rain. At the vault, there were only a couple people. Clarissa had a bag with her ..." His voice trailed off.

Dan looked at him, "Dad, thanks for telling us." He went to the sink and drew a glass of water for the judge and came back to the table setting the water in front of the judge.

The judge looked up at him, "Thanks Dan."

Dan sat down. He had to ask the next question. He looked at the judge, searching for the right words. "Was Clarissa responsible for moving the body too?"

The judge stared back at Dan, not comprehending the question ...

After several moments he said, "The body? Henry's?"

Dan nodded. He'd thought as much. The judge was in the dark about this. They all were.

September 7, 1862

Henry and Dewey had pushed hard since leaving camp. They had taken horses and ridden out past Germantown to Point-Of-Rocks. There, they'd sneaked across the Potomac river into Virginia and continued west towards Harpers Ferry. They were moving quickly, but they were used to this. They had the luxury of good rations, good equipment and for once in the war, good intelligence. They knew where Lee's forces had crossed into Maryland, and the entire Union force was on his trail. General Pope had been replaced by McClellan and the army was confident that Lee would not slip away. Although they didn't know what Lee was up to yet, they had to protect Washington and Baltimore, so they pressed forward to prevent Lee from turning eastward.

Henry had gone to his Captain with the plan that he and Dewey should head west. Henry had passed through the gap at Harpers Ferry several years before when heading west to Jasper. He knew that the gap at Harpers Ferry was a death trap. The Captain had never been there but took Henry's word on it. As Henry explained to the Captain, Lee wouldn't let his army be trapped with the Potomac behind him to the south and South Mountain to his west. He must surely be headed either north or east. Henry knew enough about tactics to be sure that the Union army would be in a position to prevent either of those routes from succeeding with whatever Lee's plans were. Henry's scheme was to head straight to Harpers Ferry as quickly as possible and await Lee's eventual retreat. When it became clearer where he would re-cross the Potomac, perhaps as far north as Williamsport. He and Dewey would be waiting. While crossing the river back into Virginia, Lee would be out in the open.

The Union garrison at Harpers Ferry would give Henry and Dewey the opportunity to resupply and get the latest information on the position of Lee's forces. Henry was sure that Lee would have to re-cross the Potomac somewhere upriver of Harpers Ferry if his forces were pushed back against South Mountain and forced around it to the north. The garrison there would not be able to move out of their fortress at the juncture of the Potomac and Shenandoah rivers. They had to stay and protect the arsenal, but they could send out scouts and relay the information quickly to McClellan.

Henry had discussed all this with Dewey while they moved west towards Harpers Ferry. Dewey was impressed that Henry had thought this through as quickly and thoroughly as he had. He was also impressed that the Captain had agreed to let them pursue Lee, off on their own. But the Captain had seen Henry in action on more than one occasion, and Dewey was sure that the Captain had seen the same look in Henry's eyes that Dewey saw so often. If Henry could get within a thousand yards of Lee, he stood a good chance of shortening the war – it was worth the gamble.

~

What Henry had no way of knowing, was that Lee had split his army into two segments. Jackson had taken two thirds of the Confederate forces, crossed over South Mountain and was planning to move against Harpers Ferry from the west. This while other elements of his force approached the heights above Harpers Ferry on both the north and the south. As Henry had said, Harpers Ferry was a death trap - and he and Dewey were headed west, straight into it.

~ *September 7, 1862* ~

Today was the wedding. It was a joyous occasion; Josiah was so handsome looking in a new suit.

Off and on during the day I thought of Henry. Where is he? Is he still alive?

~ 20 ~

Several days passed by, those that knew about the empty casket weren't discussing it much, but it was on everyone's mind. They just didn't know what to do next. The best suggestion had come from Phil. He suggested they look at the cemetery site where Henry had originally been buried. When the monument was erected, his casket had been moved to the newer granite vault that was a part of the monument. Years later, Henry's wife, Ruth, had also been interred in a separate vault that was a part of the monument.

But after discussing all this, there was little they could do. Any attempt to probe around in the cemetery would require more paperwork and somebody was sure to start asking questions. The cemetery records indicated that the spaces were unused. The spots were so far removed from the more recent interments, they had probably been forgotten about. So, for now, things at the course and at MacGregor's returned to normal. The spring golfers were now here in full force.

Susan Trasker had worked hard at MacGregor's. When she graduated from high school with her twin sister Barbara, she decided to wait and not go off to college right away. Barbara was disappointed that Susan wasn't going to college. She had thought they would perhaps go to the same school. They shared that special bond between twins that can't be explained. It has to be seen to be believed.

Instead, Susan started working for Mary at MacGregor's. Mary's longtime assistant, Betty, had decided she needed to spend more time with family and reluctantly left the restaurant. Mary and Susan had become close friends and enjoyed working together. Susan was more outgoing than Barbara, a natural for work with customers in MacGregor's. In a sense, Susan was much like Mary, having spent so much time at the course while growing up.

Teddy was proud of both his daughters but felt fortunate to have Susan nearby while Barbara was off at school. He had grown accustomed to his daughters' dating rituals, as Mary said he would. Neither girl was truly serious about any particular boyfriend. That was okay with Teddy, he'd prefer they wait a while longer – he and Mavis were in no hurry to become grandparents.

Today, Susan was working by herself in MacGregor's. Ian was practically a permanent fixture behind the bar and dourly nodded in the direction of a booth as Susan came out of the kitchen.

Susan pulled an order pad out of her apron and turned to go to the booth. As she came up past the tall, backed seat she discovered Barbara sitting there smiling back at her.

"Barb! When did you get home? You should have called!", she squealed, as Barbara stood to hug her sister. Susan looked back at Ian who was smiling broadly as he turned back down to his crossword puzzle.

Barbara said, "I wanted to come up and surprise you and daddy. Can you sit? It doesn't look too busy."

Susan plopped down next to Barbara, "Sure. Have you had lunch? I can get something for you."

Barbara said, "Thanks, but I've already eaten. How's mom and dad? I haven't seen either of them yet, I came straight up here."

Susan said, "They're fine. Mom's going to be so excited. We knew you'd be back sometime this week. Dad too. I'll go get him, if he's in his office. He may be out somewhere with Cletus."

Barbara pulled Susan's arm back down, not wanting her to leave. She said, "I wanted to talk to you first. So, how are things between you and *him*?" she said with a smile.

Susan quieted down. She looked at her sister. Quietly she said, "Not so loud."

Barbara giggled, "Come on, someone here must know by now."

Susan shook her head smiling, "I don't think so." She looked across at Ian who was still doing his puzzle.

Barbara said, "Well I don't know why you're keeping this a secret."

Susan said, "We just think it's better this way for now. You know, we're so close during the day."

While this conversation was going on, Davis Templeton, the teaching pro at the course, came into MacGregor's. The two sisters both looked back at him and smiled as he made his way over to the bar and sat down with Ian. Davis smiled over at them and said, "Afternoon ladies. Nice to see you back again Barbara."

Barbara cheerily said, "Hi Davis."

Ian looked up at Davis.

Davis turned back to him, "I've had a cancellation, so I thought I'd stop in for a coffee." He got up and poured one for himself, also offering Ian one by way of motioning with the pot.

Ian said, "Thanks, but I'm trying to cut back a little. Mary has been on my back about it. She's probably right, probably why I'm not sleeping as well as I used to."

Davis put the pot back and returned to his seat. The two sisters continued their conversation in soft voices.

Davis said to Ian, "Ian, do you think Mary will ever golf again?"

Ian straightened up and pushed his paper aside.

Davis continued, "I've been talking with Cletus off and on about this. He says Mary was a really good golfer in college but pretty much has given up on the game."

Ian said, "There's more to it than that, but yes, I don't remember the last time she played. She was so good."

Davis was thinking out loud now, "I can't imagine giving up the game. I know it's my job and all, but still – giving up the game." He shook his head not understanding.

Ian said, "Well, now with a family, and here ..." Ian waved his hand indicating MacGregor's.

Davis said, "Oh I know, her life is really full now, but ... anyway, it's too bad she doesn't play."

Davis had worked at the course for a year. He had attended college on a partial golf scholarship and done well, both in the classroom and on the team. He had also been in the Navy ROTC program at college. However, he never had quite the breakout season it took to get the attention and sponsorships to get out on the tour. But he had stayed with the game and had become an excellent teacher. Since coming to Sycamore Glen, he had steadily improved his game and was now a scratch golfer, lowering his handicap from one to zero. Maybe in the future he'd get the big break and be able to travel on the tour. But for now, he was happy at Sycamore Glen. Some of his students showed a lot of potential, he was working hard with them to try and get the best out of them. It wasn't going unnoticed. This spring, college recruiters had come to the course and talked with Davis about several students that had applied to schools based on golf scholarships. Davis had also worked with Dan and Curtis to set up a scholarship fund to try and help out some of his students.

Davis had finished his coffee. He stood up, "Well Ian, thanks for the coffee. I've got to get back out there."

Ian nodded to Davis as he left the bar, walking over to the booth where Susan and Barbara were still quietly chatting.

He came up to the booth and said, "Really Barbara, it's nice seeing you again. I hope you can make it up here once in a while. Okay? I want to find out what you've been working on in school."

Barbara nodded, "Thanks for asking. I'll try and stop by and catch up with you. If I don't see you soon, give me a call. Okay?" Susan was quiet.

"Sure." he said. "Anyway, I've got to run, I have another lesson coming up soon." With that he walked back across MacGregor's and left.

Barbara turned back towards Susan. Susan raised her eyebrows at her sister, "What's going on there?" She said as her face opened out into a broad smile.

Barbara said, "Stop, he's just being polite."

"Really" Susan said. "You've been in the classroom too much, that was more than just being polite!".

Cletus and Chip were headed back up the hill to the farmhouse. Cletus had purchased several life preservers and enough rope so they could be tied off on posts and thrown into the pond in an emergency. He just didn't trust that Katie would stay out of the water. Cletus had asked Chip to come up the hill with him. Cletus wanted to check to make sure that everything was on schedule.

Cletus pulled up to the pond and said to Chip, "I'll just be a minute or two while I pound these in. I'm putting one on each side of the pond. I know the rope won't reach out that far, but if Katie were to go in the water she wouldn't be too far from shore."

Chip got out of the cart and walked back beneath the sycamore near the outlet of the pond. Cletus had brought out a picnic table and sat it back from the water beneath the tree. The old millstones were nearby, Katie liked to play on them. Chip stood over them looking at their mammoth size. One was cracked completely across, both were laying on the ground with the furrows down into the soil. They had been here so long they had sunken down several inches into the soft soil.

Chip said to Cletus, "You know, we could probably use these stones down at MacGregor's if you don't want them up here."

Cletus came over to Chip, "Let's leave them here for now. Besides, these things would be tough to move. They look even bigger than any of the stones down in the mill, don't they?"

Chip looked down at them. These were huge stones. He said to Cletus, "The mill up here much have been gigantic to have used stones this big."

Cletus motioned Chip back to the cart. He moved around the pond closer to the farmhouse and put in a second preserver and post, hanging the preserver from the post after he'd driven it down firmly into the ground. When he finished, they drove across to the farm house.

Mary and Katie were there. The painting had ended, and several rooms had been wallpapered. With the power now on, the telephone connected, and the furnace running, about the only thing left to do was move all the contents of the apartment up into the farmhouse.

Today was Monday and they had decided to move on the least busiest day of the week, Wednesday. This was a final check by Mary and Chip, that the move could happen as planned.

Cletus came in through the front door to find Mary and Katie looking around the room.

Mary said, "Well I think we're all done here."

Chip looked around, walked into the kitchen, and came back out. "Yeah, it looks nice. I can't think of anything else. What about you Cletus?"

Cletus nodded, "It looks great in here. I can't thank you enough Chip, for everything you've done."

Mary agreed, "Cletus is right. I don't know how we'd have managed this without you."

Chip was embarrassed. All he could say was, "Well it was my pleasure. I know you're going to be happy up here. I've come to love it up here myself, you know, the pond and all."

Mary looked at Cletus, Cletus nodded to her, 'go ahead'.

She said, "Chip, there's something else up here you could help us out with."

Chip looked at Mary, "Sure, what do you need."

Mary continued, "Well you know when Dan purchased the farm up here it was for a couple reasons. He knew we'd be able to move in up here without a lot of trouble, which would help you free up space in the clubhouse for everything to start happening down there."

Chip nodded.

Mary went on, "He also wanted the land to create another 18-hole course, further down the hill alongside the existing course."

Chip nodded again.

Mary said, "Well he had another reason also. He's going to be putting up several homes up here near us, and Dick will also buy a couple lots for some homes."

Chip hadn't really heard about any of this before.

Cletus chimed in, "But we told Dan we had ideas for a home up here also."

Chip was confused now. He looked back at Mary, he didn't understand. They were all set to move into their new home …

Mary saw the confused look on Chip's face, "We asked Dan to set aside a lot, right next to us here." She motioned out the side window. "For our first neighbor – you."

Chip was still confused. "I don't understand …"

Cletus said, "It's simple. You're 'remodeling' yourself out of your home. I know Dan said the job would last two or three years, but everyone thinks this should be a permanent position."

Mary came over to him, "Chip you're a dear, you're family, we want you close by. We all do. Dan knew he'd be terrible at this, so he asked us to bring you up here and explain everything. He's had his hands full – as you know."

Cletus continued, "Dick's going to be stopping by with a variety of plans to look over. If any of them strike your fancy, tell him so. I think Dick and Dan have worked out a deal for a home in exchange for some land, so this can happen pretty quickly, depending on Dick's work load. But he has several crews so I'm sure this isn't a big deal for him to make happen – maybe in line with the schedule for work happening in the clubhouse."

Chip started to say something, but couldn't finish, "I don't know ..."

Mary interrupted him, "Well, we can finish this conversation in MacGregor's. I've got to get Katie fed and I'm sure you two are hungry. So, come on, let's have some lunch." With that Mary headed out, with Katie in tow, to her cart. Cletus and Chip followed in his cart as the caravan made its way around the pond, down the hill.

While they were in the cart, Cletus said to Chip, "I'm going to let you in on a little secret Chip."

Chip looked at Cletus.

Smiling at Chip he said, "Don't argue with Mary or Dan, it's pointless." Then he said, "Welcome to Sycamore Hill – neighbor!"

~ 22 ~

Chip didn't waste any time tracking down Dan. After having lunch with Mary and Cletus, he found Dan in his office. Dan looked up when Chip knocked at the door and waved him in.

Dan finished the paperwork as Chip sat down.

"What's up? What do you need?"

Chip said, "Nothing Dan, I'm fine. I just wanted to come in and talk to you about what's going on up on the hill."

Dan leaned back in his chair, "There's no problem up there is there?"

Chip smiled, "No Dan everything's fine. I just don't know what to say to you. I can't thank you ..."

Dan cut him off, "No thanks necessary Chip. This will all work out nicely – for everyone. The truth is that none of this could really happen without you. I've got my hands full with the course, well ... everyone's got their hands full with their work here. You, too. But you're moving us forward. When all these changes are done, this place will really be something. I know we don't have a lot of tangible results yet, but once you start in on the restaurant and pub, you'll see. I can't wait."

Chip had listened, "Well Dan, I still owe you a lot for bringing me on here. Everyone has been terrific. I just wanted you to know that it means a great deal to me."

Dan stood up and came around his desk. He put his hand on Chip's shoulder. "Listen son, you just keep doing what you're doing, everything will work out. I know you're chomping at the bit to get going in the mill building. After Mary and Cletus move – it's all yours."

"Come on, let me buy you a coffee, we have to get caught up with Ian – he's just as anxious as you to get started in there." Dan nodded toward the older portion of the building as he led Chip out towards MacGregor's.

September 14, 1862

As Henry and Dewey moved out of Harpers Ferry, they kept a close eye on the Maryland heights above the Potomac river. The rebels were moving cannon up the hill. Once they were in place, the fight would be over. They didn't know it, but Jackson had sealed off everything west of the ferry. He and his foot cavalry had swung around South Mountain to move in on Harpers Ferry from the west. It was also apparent that there were cannon moving into position above the Shenandoah river on Louden heights to the south of the ferry. It was a classic pincers movement by Jackson, attacking the ferry simultaneously from three directions.

What concerned Henry, was that Jackson had gotten into position behind Harpers Ferry so quickly. He must have crossed South Mountain at one or more of the gaps. This must have been Lee's plan, all along. It meant Lee wasn't far off. Maybe he had crossed South Mountain too. What Henry knew was that he and Dewey had to get upriver quickly to intercept Lee, if it was possible to get past Jackson's forces before the attack on Harpers Ferry began. Henry and Dewey had tagged along with a force of about 1,300 men led by Colonel Benjamin Davis, who was determined to save the men from entrapment and capture at Harpers Ferry. They had moved out ahead of Henry and Dewey as they tried to get out in front of the Confederate forces, not knowing exactly where the rest of Lee's army was.

Henry and Dewey were being cautious, but speed also counted. He motioned Dewey to come up with him, away from the river a little more, where the undergrowth wasn't as thick. There were sycamores here, not unlike those back in the Glen. Henry had to force his mind back into the present.

"We best move along a bit faster or they'll start shooting." Henry said quietly to Dewey when he joined him.

Dewey craned his head back to look up. "Not possible Henry, the musket rounds would just fall back out of the barrels before they fired."

Henry chuckled. You had to admire the optimism of Dewey.

"On the other hand, Henry, they could just roll rocks down on us to kill us."

Henry's only comment was, "Well, let's get a move on before they figure that out, or before you or some other genius up on that hill can come up with any other brilliant ways to kill us."

~ 23 ~

The move went smoothly on Wednesday. It seemed that everybody wanted to help. At times Mary and Cletus felt like bystanders as everybody bustled about carrying boxes, lamps and all manner of objects. The two of them spent more time explaining where things went, than actually moving anything themselves. Katie had been left with "Poppy" to help manage MacGregor's while nearly everyone else pitched in at either the top or bottom of Sycamore Hill.

As the moving crew finished their efforts near dinnertime, everyone came back down to the patio at the clubhouse for a meal that Susan had put together. She could see that Mary looked beat. Mary had been under orders from Cletus, and everyone else, to not overdo it. She was into the second trimester of her pregnancy and was habitually tired. This wasn't progressing as her pregnancy with Katie had. Her doctor had assured her and Cletus that everything was normal, 'Not every pregnancy followed the same course.' He told her on several occasions.

Claire and Mary were quietly talking at one end of a table while Cletus, Dan, Chip and Teddy were in deep conversation at the other end of the table. As Mary and Claire finishing chatting for a moment, Mary caught Cletus' attention and nodded to him.

Cletus stood up. His voice didn't boom out like Dan's would have, but everyone understood he had something to say, "Everyone. Mary and I want to say thanks for helping with the move. We couldn't have done it without you. I don't think anything got broken, and I'm sure we'll find everything that was moved – sometime – after we find the right box it's in." There was some laughter. "But we want to invite all of you up to the top of the hill as soon as we're unpacked and settled. You'll always be welcome, you're our family." Mary smiled at Cletus as he sat down.

Dan stood. "As long as we have everyone together, I thought I'd pass on a little news. Teddy and I have convinced Chip, here, to stay on as the permanent construction manager for Sycamore Glen. We have a number of things we'd like to accomplish besides the renovations that Chip is starting on at the clubhouse, now that the 'tenants' have moved out." There was a little laughter at this as he continued. "I know we told Chip this was only for a couple of years when we first got together, but everyone here feels it's a lot more than that. It's probably not a secret to anyone here that we'll be adding another 18 holes in the next year or so. That means we'll all have plenty to do around here, but it also means we'll have some more stability in our lives in the off season when there's no golfing going on. I think there will be enough to do during the off season, and with the course doing so well, we'd like to keep everyone working straight through the winter if they're able to." There was some applause at this. "We've got a lot of talented people gathered here," continued Dan, "With MacGregor's operating all year, and with other things we have in mind, Sycamore Glens' future looks great and I just wanted to let everybody know how we felt about that." As Dan motioned for Claire to join him.

"Dan's right.", said Claire as she stood beside Dan. "Cletus is right, we're a family here, and we want to keep it that way. The Judge always felt that way, he still does. He wanted me to say that he was sorry that he couldn't make it here. I know he felt like he should be helping with the move, but he is just feeling a little under the weather, so I convinced him not to come. Anyway, Mary, Cletus – we all know you'll love your new home. We'll miss seeing you every time we turn around here in the clubhouse or out on the course. But you have a beautiful home up on the hill and it's not that far away from your home down here." As she finished, there were more than a few teary-eyed people seated at the tables.

After Claire sat down some of the people drifted off to head home for the evening. Most stopped to say goodbye to Mary or Cletus. It had been a long day, and most would be back tomorrow bright and early. Before anyone had left his table, Teddy stood up and said, "Before everyone takes off, I just wanted to invite everyone here to Johnnie's on Sunday night at about seven. I think you all know that Barbara's home now and Mavis and I wanted to give everyone a chance to say hi to her before she's gone again before starting her next semester. I know she has some plans, but I'll let her tell you all about it then. If you could join us, we'd appreciate it. If you can make it, let me know, Nancy and Russell are going to join us too."

On their way home, up the hill, for the first time, Cletus asked Mary, "So what's Barbara up to? Has Susan said anything?"

Mary said, "No. She's been pretty tight lipped about it. But you know how it is with sisters, especially twins. They're in their own little world sometimes. Barbara is Susan's closest friend. I know she misses her terribly when she's away at school. We'll find out Sunday night."

While Claire and Dan were headed down the hill on their way home, Claire said to Dan, "Dan I'm going to the bank tomorrow with Dad. We're going to open the safety deposit box. It's time. He's ready for it. I think he'll feel better after we do it."

Dan just nodded. He felt the same way too. He could see the Judge going downhill over the past several months. This would help him. Dan didn't think the Judge was physically failing, but Dan could sense him slipping in other ways. This had eaten away at the Judge for fifty years – it was finally beginning to have an outward effect on him.

~ 24 ~

The next morning Claire came to the Judge's house at about the time he normally ate breakfast. She tapped at the kitchen door and entered to find the Judge eating his bowl of Cheerios. Claire couldn't help but chuckle as she sat down. A former judge slurping down a bowl of Cheerios like some grade schooler.

The Judge smiled across at her. "Hey, even ex Judges like Cheerios. Just give me a minute or two and we'll get over to the bank."

Claire watched as the Judge got up, moved to the sink with his cereal bowl then off to get a coat from the hallway closet. He was back in a minute. Ready to go. She felt good about this, he was behaving more positively than she'd seen him in the last week or so.

They left the house walking down the back steps towards Claire's car. The Judge stopped on the sidewalk. "Claire lets walk. It's not that far, it's a nice morning for a walk."

Claire turned back from her car, and as she came back to the Judge, put her hand through his crooked arm, walking beside him toward the bank.

It only took ten minutes to reach the bank, even walking at the Judge's slower, but deliberate, pace. It was a gorgeous late spring morning. Most of the homes they passed still had tulips and daffodils in bloom in their gardens. The lawns had already been mown several times this year. It was a spring like most others - beautiful.

When they entered the bank, everyone noticed. Most said 'Hi' if they were within range of the Judge's hearing. He acknowledged everyone, as he always did. There was enough attention by everyone that the manager, Steven Wainwright, became aware and came out of his office to greet Claire and the Judge.

He said, "Good morning Mayor Steele, Judge Osborn. Beautiful out there isn't it?"

Claire said, "Morning Steven, how many times do I have to ask you to call me Claire?" She said in a teasing tone.

The Judge chuckled. Claire would always be Claire, mayor or not. Everyone knew that, even Steven. The Judge suspected it was more than respect when someone addressed her as Mayor Steele, they wanted her to know she would always be 'more' than just – Claire.

"Steven, the Judge would like to access his safety deposit box." Claire said as she held out his key to Steven. "It hasn't been opened in a while."

Steven said, "That's not a problem, whenever you need access, we're always here. Please, follow me to the vault." He looked at the number on the key and handed it back to Claire.

They continued back further into the bank. Steven lead them through a set of gated doors into a small corridor lined with safety deposit boxes of different sizes. After looking at the numbers on the boxes stacked row upon row, he stopped and withdrew his master key which he turned in a lock, then stepped aside for Claire to use the key the Judge had given her. She opened the door and withdrew a large cubic box.

Steven said, "If you follow me back down the other side of the corridor, we have several private rooms - if you'd like to use one of them." Claire and the Judge followed. As they entered one of the rooms, Steven said, "There's a desk and other items you may need, as well as a phone. I'll leave you in private, would you like some coffee, or perhaps some water?"

Claire said to him, "Thank you Steven I think we've got everything we need."

Steven continued, "Well, if you need anything just pick up the phone and dial 7, that's my extension. Stay as long as you like, I'll be in my office if you need anything else, okay?"

The Judge spoke, "Thank you Steven, we won't be long."

Steven nodded and left.

Claire sat down beside the Judge at the desk, waiting for him to open the box.

The Judge lifted the cover and pulled out a somewhat smaller box. It was a tarnished silver-plated box. It was probably quite decorative looking when new. Now it was hard to make out all the scrollwork down on edges and on the corners.

"It looks smaller and heavier now than what I remember stuffing in that huge bag of Clarissa's"

As Claire watched her father closely, tears were starting to form in the corner of his eyes.

He pushed the box in front of Claire. He said, "This is for you to do, not me. This isn't about me, it's about Jasper, it's about our community, you should be the one to look inside."

Claire understood, this was the 'Judge' in her father coming forward, as he had all throughout her life.

She lifted the lid carefully. The box was strong, the lid heavy, as she lifted it fully open and let it down gently against the back of the box. She looked inside and saw that it was nearly filled with a variety of items.

She slid the box back towards her father so they could explore the contents together. As she suspected, most of the items she saw were mentioned in some of the articles she'd read about the ceremony. She began taking them out and laying them carefully on the desk. While the box wasn't big enough for a complete newspaper, there were several sections of newspaper that had been rolled up tightly and tied with twine. On one of the rolls, the twine had broken, and the roll popped open somewhat. It had stayed tied for enough time that the roll had kept most of its shape after the twine had broken.

There were some political buttons and a ribbon from the county fair that must have held some significance. There were several neatly written pages – probably like what the school was planning on putting back in the 'capsule' when it was resealed. There were several smaller items, the judge chuckled when he saw them.

Finally, lying flat in the bottom of the box, and almost as big as the box was an ornately bound book with a single word on its cover … 'Diary'.

September 18, 1862

Henry and Dewey had reached their position along the Potomac riverbank during the middle of the night. At daybreak on the 18th, they studied the opposite, Virginia side, of the river, looking for any sign of movement. It wasn't long before a group of four cannons with their crews set up in an opening just upstream of where Henry and Dewey lay hidden in the undergrowth. The cannons were splayed out to cover a sizeable portion of the riverbank – including where Henry and Dewey lay hidden. Henry could just make out another emplacement being put together several hundred yards further upstream. It had been difficult to choose "the" spot they should occupy when they had arrived in the early morning hours. Henry had looked out into the darkness and listened for the sound of shallow water at Packhorse Ford. He couldn't hear any, the river was running a little higher than normal for this time of the year. He had settled on this position because he could look both upstream and downstream quite nicely from the small prominence they were positioned on. They were far enough from the ford, such that, the sentries at the ford hadn't spotted them.

As the day wore on, there was more movement upstream, but only a small number of soldiers were making the crossing, surely no senior officers. This was all about establishing a force to protect the real retreat, that would probably occur under the cover of darkness. Henry was gambling that Lee would either cross early in the evening when it was still light – in effect leading his men home to safety.

Or, he would cross near the end of his column, ensuring that his men had all made it across safely, before he went across into Virginia. If this were the case, Henry hoped that the crossing would take long enough to cause Lee to make the crossing the next morning when there might be enough light to spot him crossing the river.

Towards nightfall more troops came across the river, some now on horseback. Henry was losing the light. He had to hope Lee would cross the next morning. As the evening deepened, torches were lit by the retreating rebels, riders held them in place along the route across the river. While the light aided those crossing the river, it wasn't good enough to help Henry or Dewey identify their intended target.

Neither Henry nor Dewey got much sleep. They were close to the crossing, and twice, men on horseback had ridden behind them. While they were close on the riverbank, immediately behind them was a depression that had been a busy canal until the war broke out. This small portion was dry, as the embankment that ran alongside the river had been damaged in several places but not yet repaired. So far, no one had ventured along the narrow berm between the canal bed and the river. It was thickly covered with undergrowth and small trees that had grown up when the maintenance along the canal had stopped as the war raged on.

~ 25 ~

Dan was in his office when there was a soft knock at the door. "Come on in, it's open." He bellowed out, as usual.

Teddy poked his head in. Before he could say anything to Dan, Dan began, "You are just the person I hoped I would see." Dan caught himself from charging forward – "Sorry, what I can do for you. You look like this is more than something about running a golf course. Sit down."

Teddy plopped down on the couch across from Dan's desk. A smile was coming to his face. "No problem, I actually feel a little better just since 'encountering' you. It's infectious."

Dan came around from his desk and sat back against the edge of it. "Really Teddy, what's up? We can talk."

Teddy hesitated, "Well, I've had a lot on my mind lately, it probably shows, I know I haven't seemed like myself at times."

Dan laughed, "You mean there's more going on with you than, running a golf course, twelve or fourteen hours a day, driving almost an hour each way to get here - then home, trying to keep some sort of life together with your beautiful wife, and, oh, yeah I almost forgot – watch over your two gorgeous girls who are dating and probably driving you crazy during the rest of your free time."

Teddy was now smiling widely at Dan. "You don't miss much around here, do you?"

Dan just smiled.

Teddy continued, "Between you and Ian there can't be many secrets around here, can there?"

Dan continuing smiling, challenging Teddy to continue.

"Well I'm just learning about something. And I'm not really surprised. I'm not angry. I'm actually a little pleased. But mostly I'm just curious."

Now Dan was interested. He leaned forward a little, from his position against the desk – waiting.

Teddy was still smiling, searching for the right words to use next. "Did you ...have any idea ...of what was going on ...between Susan and Chip?"

Dan snapped back a little, "Yes! Give that man a stuffed animal for guessing correctly!"

Teddy was laughing now. Of course, Dan knew.

Dan stood up, reaching out to Teddy, "Come on, let's go have a coffee and see if Ian also knew. It's Susan's day off so this could really be fun."

With that, the two of them headed off towards MacGregor's.

~ 26 ~

Claire and the Judge had returned the objects to the ornate box and placed it back into the safety deposit box. Calling Steven to come back, together they relocked the box. The Judge thanked Steven, as did Claire and together they left the bank - with the diary in Claire's briefcase. They walked back towards the square, the Judge asked Claire to sit with him on one of the park benches that were scattered about the perimeter of the park.

As they sat, the judge turned to his daughter and said, "You have no idea how relieved I am."

She studied him, smiling as she said, "You see, we told you this was not something to worry about. Everything looks to be intact. Regardless of Clarissa's motives, it was probably a good thing to leave it stored in the bank. Moisture could have gotten in there at the monument. It could have even been broken into and damaged or stolen."

At the mention of the vault being broken into, the judge snapped back into the moment. "Claire, what really happened with the vault? What do you suppose is going on with all this.?"

Claire tried to keep a positive attitude towards 'all this' as she said, "Dad, let me spend some time with the diary, if you don't mind me reading it?"

The Judge hoped Claire would suggest this. He said, "Claire, I'd appreciate that. I don't know what we'll find in there, but it should be you doing the discovering. I never knew much about the family, except what little Clarissa passed on to me. It's best you start out fresh on your own with this. I know I never said much about your grandparents, and their parents, but, well, you read the diary. Hopefully it will fill in a lot of blanks."

Claire looked across the green expanse to the statue. Wondering more about Henry. Who was he - really?

September 19, 1862

early morning

Approaching dawn, there were still troops crossing in the shallow water of the ford. Henry strained to look at the soldiers that were on horseback, was Lee one of them? During the night, wagons had made the crossing. Although the men had obviously been given orders to stay quiet while retreating, you couldn't help but hear muted cries of pain from the wounded.

Quietly Henry nudged Dewey and motioned toward the ford. "I think it's him." Was all Henry said. He repositioned the Whitworth against his shoulder to quickly take aim. There might only be one shot. As he lightly squeezed the trigger, Lee's horse, Traveller, stumbled slightly but recovered without spilling Lee into the river. The sound of the errant shot echoed off the riverbanks. There had been other sporadic shots. But this one sounded different, the distinctive whistling of the hexagonal round. Louder, maybe more deliberant than other shots, that sounded like they had been fired upwards – the echo sounding solid, purposeful.

"Damn it, his horse stumbled." Henry said. Dewey was already squeezing down on his trigger. His shot hit the horse of the man riding alongside Lee. The horse buckled and toppled into the water taking his rider with him. Those nearby rushed to pull the officer out of the water and hurry Lee along also.

Henry was almost done reloading while Dewey, with his breech loading Sharps, was already taking aim again, trying to find Lee in the melee along the ford near the Virginia shore. His shot completely missed this time but caused several of those near Lee to turn in their direction.

As Henry squinted through the scope on the Whitworth, a shot rang out in their direction and hit only yards away. Henry had seen the muzzle flash and in a reflexive action, shifted his aim and killed the marksman.

Lee was up the bank now, out of sight in the crowd lining the shore.

Other rifle fire started up. Some of it hitting close to their position.

Henry laid down quickly and said to Dewey, "Stop firing, get down, it's over."

~ 27 ~

Back at McGregor's, Dan and Teddy were enjoying a coffee with Ian. Of course, Ian had known about Susan and Chip. Having watched Susan grow up, it was no surprise that she would be the one to stay settled at home rather than leave to go to school. As much as the two sisters were alike, and as close as they were, neither had divulged much about their boyfriends to anyone. Ian had seen Mary dating boys when she was their age. Mary was so much more outgoing than either Susan or Barbara. When Mary had gone off to school, and particularly after the death of Kate, she had retreated somewhat into her own little world which had bothered Ian. It just didn't seem right.

Ian had watched Susan go through some of the same behavior. As she immersed herself at McGregor's, the stream of boyfriends tapered off. He was concerned but kept it to himself. After Chip began working at the course, Susan changed, small things at first, but she was different. She was maturing, she had taken control of her life. She was falling in love.

He told Teddy as much. Teddy had missed so much of the girls' lives – working long hours at the course. He now realized how right Mavis had been about trying to spend more time with the girls. Teddy said to Ian, "It's probably some curse. First you can't wait to see them off to school – then all you want is for them to be closer. I don't understand it."

Ian chuckled, "'Life' is the word you're looking for."

Dan laughed, "You two are the luckiest guys around here, and look at you. Trying to 'understand' everything. Just let it happen. Enjoy it. I know I am. I'm everybody's 'Uncle' and I'm having a ball."

Teddy and Ian had to laugh at this. Teddy said, "Well 'Uncle' Dan, if Claire were a little younger, you might be singing a different tune."

Ian was laughing also when Dan said to him, "Claire and I have talked about adopting, but ..." Dan let it end at that.

Ian stopping laughing and added, "You'd be a great parent, Claire too. Is this serious? Are you two going to go through with it?"

Dan said, "Let's keep it quiet a little longer. We're still just discussing it, nothing more. I don't want to put anything else on Claire's plate just now. We'll see."

Teddy added, "How's the judge? I thought he and Claire were going to look in the box? What's going on there.?"

Dan said, "Yeah they're at the bank this morning. I hope it all goes okay. Claire said she'd stop up here after they've looked over everything. She should be along anytime."

While they were talking, Mary came into the restaurant with Cletus. Cletus had been at the course since dawn but was joining Mary while she had a late breakfast.

Ian said to them as they approached, "Morning Mary, Cletus. Big day today – Katie's first day at the day care center. How was she handling it this morning?"

Mary said, "She got me up this morning, so she wouldn't be late. She'll take the place by storm. I hope they're ready for her."

Dan was laughing, "And whooooom did she inherit that from might I ask?"

Mary had to laugh, "That must have been soooo difficult to figure out." She passed by him and gave him a quick kiss on his cheek as she went into the kitchen.

Dan turned back around to Cletus who had sat down beside him, "Hey there lover-boy, do you let your wife go around kissing everyone like that?"

"Morning Dan", said Cletus as he nodded in thanks to Ian who was sliding a coffee in front of Cletus. Cletus said to Dan, "Well, the last person I saw her kiss like that ...", he paused for effect, "became my boss! I'm still not sure about the effect one might have had on the other.", and he shook his head.

Teddy was laughing, "I'll give you some advice that a wise person once gave me – 'Don't try to understand everything. Just let it happen. Enjoy it.' "

~ 28 ~

Dan and Ian were still at the bar when Claire came into MacGregor's. She sat next to Dan.

Ian said, "Morning Claire."

Claire was smiling, "Morning Ian."

Dan looked at her with a 'So?' expression.

Claire said, "Well it went okay. Dad's feeling a lot better. No big surprises in the box. Pretty much what we thought we'd find. Everything looks to be intact."

Ian said, "So, no clues as to what really happened out there?"

Claire said, "The only surprise was a diary that Clarissa added to the box. I've brought it with me. I thought dad would want to read it first, but he told me to take it. I think he's just relieved that the 'big secret' is out in the open."

Dan agreed, "So he took it okay?"

Claire smiled, "Yes, he's okay with it."

Ian said, "So what's next? How are you going to handle things in July?"

Claire had thought quite a bit about this, depending on what was in the time capsule, "Well, I think we shouldn't change anything. We'll tell everyone what was in the capsule. We can say that the diary is part of our family history, and we'd like to read it first. It may be able to answer some questions about Henry. It might help provide some history about Jasper that's been lost. We've got some time. I'll read it, dad and I can see what's in it."

Dan had been quiet, finally he spoke, "Well just take it slow with dad, okay?"

Claire nodded.

Ian said to them, "I've got a little history to read up on myself. I've been going through the ledgers that Chip found over in the mill. Some of the names are familiar, others aren't. Most of the transactions are after the war. Maybe some of it will tie in with the diary. Back then the community was a lot smaller, but close knit. I'd bet that the mill was the center of a lot of activity, not just for the milling. It stayed pretty busy even after most of the milling shifted over to Bingley where a more modern mill had been built.

Chip and I have been looking over the machinery in the basement and it looks as though the mill was converted over into a good-sized machine shop when the milling operations ceased."

September 19, 1862

afternoon

Henry and Dewey had stayed quiet for several hours while the rifle fire died down, then stopped. It had been over an hour since the last shot. The soldiers were now all across the river at the ford. The cannons were still in place. Obviously, the Union troops would come up to pursue Lee. What was taking them so long?

Not long after those thoughts had crossed Henry's mind, a small detachment of Union troops came up quietly from the dry canal bed that was behind Henry and Dewey. They were startled to find anyone there ahead of them.

A Lieutenant crouched down alongside Henry, "Who the hell are you soldier? What are you doing here?"

Henry said to him, "That's a damn fool question, I'm trying to fight a war here. …Sir."

The Lieutenant looked at Henry, "Sergeant what unit are you with?"

Henry said, "118th Pennsylvania Infantry sir, Colonel Provost commanding. He sends his regards sir."

This brought a slight smile to the Lieutenants face. "Seems like you men got out in front of us just a bit."

Dewey looked at him and smiled, "Just a bit. Sir."

The Lieutenant said, "Well, you're with us now Corporal. You and the Sergeant, here, fall in and we'll be crossing the river up there at the ford when everyone is up."

Dewey looked at Henry. Henry said to the Lieutenant, "Sir, we're detached from our unit with orders that require us to hold our position here."

The Lieutenant looked at Henry, "I'm countermanding those orders. You'll join us and cross the river on my command."

Henry said, "Begging your pardon sir, but we can't disobey our orders. They come from the division headquarters. With all due respect sir."

The Lieutenant was starting to get a little angry. But the Sergeant was polite. He was in no rush to enter the river without everyone behind him in position.

Henry could see the trouble the Lieutenant was having and said, "If I might suggest sir, perhaps we could move back a bit, maybe into the depression behind us and discuss this a little further? The cannon crew across the river is just about ready to send a round our way. Corporal Carson, would you be so kind as to forestall that Sergeant with the lanyard on the other side of the river from interrupting the conversation I'm trying to have with the Lieutenant?"

Dewey had been watching the cannon crew also. It only took him a moment to act upon Henry's suggestion. When the shot rang out it startled the Lieutenant. They watched as the soldier on the far side of the river fell to the ground.

The Lieutenant stared at Dewey then saw the Sharps he was holding. He turned back to Henry and studied the Whitworth. The wheels were churning in the Lieutenant's mind.

Henry spoke, "Thank you Corporal Carson. Now sir, you're putting me in an awkward position. I mean no disrespect sir, but I think Corporal Carson and I should stay put here for a while longer. As much as we would enjoy invading Virginia with you and your fine troopers here behind us, I really think we should obey the previous orders we've been given. Corporal Carson, that group across the river is persistent. It seems as though they've elected someone new to pull the lanyard. If you would, perhaps, curb their enthusiasm regarding our presence here ..." Dewey's shot cut Henry off from finishing the sentence.

The Lieutenant flinched a little then looked across the river as another soldier was falling to the ground.

Henry continued, "Now sir, perhaps I have a suggestion that will solve our problem here. Suppose, when your men are all up here, Corporal Carson and I, cover your men while they cross the river? Corporal Carson is just about the finest shot in the army. I know he's the best shot I've ever seen."

Dewey smiled as he looked up at the Lieutenant. The Lieutenant looked down at him and said, "Son you are without question the best shot I've ever seen, also. I tend to agree with the Sergeant here, that it might make more sense for you and your Sergeant, to cover our crossing from this position."

Henry said to the Lieutenant, "Sir it does appear that we have a problem on the far riverbank. It seems as though our conversation here has drawn some attention, and they do appear to be shifting the position of another of their cannon somewhat in our direction."

Dewey smiled and looked at Henry saying, "Sarge, do you suppose one of their cannons over there might be spiked? If it were, the Lieutenant here might have a chance to reorganize his men that are arriving, for the push across the river, while those cannoneers over there decide what to do next."

Henry returned the smile. As he looked through his scope at one of the cannons, the loader was bringing a charge towards the muzzle. When Henry's shot rang out, there was an almost immediate explosion on the far side of the river, and even the men behind the Lieutenant flinched.

The Lieutenant looked down at Henry, then Dewey. He had just seen *two* of the finest shooters in the army in action.

~ 29 ~

It was late in June. School had been over with for a couple of weeks and all the summer workers were hard at work at the golf course. Business there was booming, as was the business at MacGregor's. The patio seating was full, from lunchtime until after the course closed each day. Tee times were hard to come by. Most golfers made reservations a week in advance – even for weekdays. Golf in general was thriving. In the spring, Jack Nicklaus won the Masters golf tournament for the first time. The rivalry with Arnold Palmer had energized the public interest in the sport. Everyone wanted to play golf.

Dan couldn't have chosen a better time to expand Sycamore Glen. He was even approached by investors who wanted to put their money in a business that was obviously flourishing. He was flattered and appreciative but kept the business in the hands of his wife, Claire, and himself. He wasn't trying to make a fortune for himself and Claire, he was just as concerned about the community. He tried to keep the course as he had discovered it – a fun place to come, where everyone was treated like family. If he could provide more income for the community by drawing people to the course, then everyone prospered.

It was a cloudless Saturday morning, just past six thirty, when Dan came into MacGregor's for his first coffee of the day. Ian was helping take breakfast orders until two more waitresses scheduled to work came in at seven. Ian nodded to Dan as Dan was pouring his coffee, then came back to sit at the bar.

As Ian came back out of the kitchen after depositing several orders, he came up to the window and looked out at the course. He turned to Dan, "Already a backup on the first tee."

Dan came over and looked out. It didn't surprise him, there were quite a few cars in the lot. As they looked at the practice green, he said to Ian, "It's going to be busy around here today, hot too."

Ian said, "I've got everyone coming in today, we're going to be jumping all day."

Dan smiled, "You wouldn't want it any other way, would you?"

Ian smiled back, "No." said Ian as he headed back into the kitchen.

As the swinging door swung back into place, Mary came through with a full tray of breakfasts. She nodded to Dan as she passed behind him.

"Morning, Mrs. Armstrong." was his simple greeting.

Looking back towards the number 1 tee box Dan saw Curtis with the starter. They were scanning the area watching the slow buildup of golfers.

A couple minutes later Mary came back through, "Your husband out there already this morning?", Dan said.

Mary looked at him, "Yes, I believe he is attempting to keep this place in pristine shape for the hoard of hackers that seems to have attacked us today." She said with a smile as she passed back into the kitchen.

As Ian returned, Dan quietly said to him, "I'd like a word with you later when it's calmed down a bit, nothing urgent." He tapped the bar lightly with the knuckles on his right hand as he raised it in a casual salute and left the pub to talk with Curtis down on the first tee.

Ian nodded, but stood there for a moment wondering what was really on Dan's mind this morning.

~

When Dan reached Curtis, there were three groups milling around the tee box. He said to Curtis, "Bit of a logjam this morning Curtis?"

Curtis smiled as he responded, "No sir. These three groups are together. Came down from Syracuse. They're just waiting for their first group to go off."

"Ah" said Dan, "Just a little interest in each other's tee shots. Probably a little money riding on the outcome. Eh boys?"

They came over to Dan. Curtis introduced him, "Gentlemen, meet Mr. Steele, the owner of Sycamore Glen."

Dan shook hands, as he did, he corrected Curtis – "The name's Dan, gents. Hope you like the course. First time here?"

The golfer closest to Dan nodded yes, "Heard about this place from a friend. The drive out here wasn't too bad. Looks like you have a nice layout here."

Dan nodded in agreement, "It'll challenge you. It's got a little something for everybody. You boy's staying over for some golf tomorrow too?"

There was some nodding, apparently, they really hadn't thought about it much.

"Well if you do, I can promise you some easier pin placements tomorrow. We change 'em on Sunday morning to give you a different look on the weekends. I guarantee they'll be easier tomorrow."

They were laughing now. Even Curtis had to chuckle, Dan was still a salesman.

"You boys have had some good teams at Syracuse over the past couple years. Who's your running back this year? Who's wearing 44?"

"Bill Schoonover" was the unanimous response.

Dan looked puzzled, "Sorry, don't know much about him." He paused for a moment, "Too bad about Ernie Davis. He was something special. He would'a made it big in the pros."

There was agreement on that from everyone. Dick, the person getting ready to tee off said, "We've got a freshman, Floyd Little, I hear he may be someone to watch next year."

"I will." Dan replied. "Well listen, you boys have fun out there. Watch yourself on 14. That creek on the dogleg will play hell with your score. Make sure you stay for the cookout tonight. We're having some steaks out here on the barbecue pit – you won't be disappointed." Dan nodded to Curtis and walked off towards the practice green, curious as to who he might know over there.

Ian had watched from his perch in MacGregor's, Dan really was someone fun to watch when he was on his game.

~ 30 ~

Dan came into MacGregor's at about three that afternoon. He looked around and saw that the lunchtime crowd had thinned considerably. Bruce was working with Ian at the bar. Most of the business was happening down on the patio.

Ian had seen Dan come in. He mentioned to Bruce he'd be with Dan for a bit. If it suddenly got busy, he'd rejoin him at the bar. Ian moved out from the bar and motioned Dan to a booth. As they sat, Ian said, "What's on your mind Dan?"

Dan was trying to use the right words, "The thing is Ian, I'm thinking of changing a couple things around here."

Ian was watching Dan closely.

They were seated where you could look out at the course. Dan looked out. He pointed out at the course. "See him out there."

Ian looked, Dan was pointing at Cletus. Ian nodded, "Cletus?" he asked.

"Yup" said Dan. "Claire and I have been talking a lot about this recently."

"Cletus?" said Ian again.

Dan smiled, "Well no, not exactly."

Ian was confused, and it showed.

Dan began again, "You know that Claire and I have been thinking about adopting?"

Ian nodded, "Seems like I heard something about that, probably from Mary. You're not thinking of adopting him, are you?", pointing out at Cletus.

Dan had to laugh at that, "Him? No, never."

Ian was still lost.

Dan said, "We're probably too old to adopt. Who knows? We may go forward with it, maybe not. I think we both are interested, but ..."

Ian said, "You two would be great parents – and, you're not too old. Don't think that."

Dan said, "Well maybe that doesn't have anything to do with this."

Ian just sat there.

"Ian, we want to make sure Mary, Katie and Cletus out there ..." he said nodding out the window, "will have Sycamore Glen."

"We can't have you or Mary paying rent for anything here anymore. This is your home. Claire and I are just 'overseeing' the course. Look at him out there."

Ian looked at Cletus again.

"He's as much the heart of this course as Mary is the soul of MacGregor's. You and I aren't getting any younger. They're running all of this." He said as he waved his hand outward in a gesture encompassing everything around them.

Dan continued, "We don't have to say anything to them yet, I just wanted you to know. I don't want them to change how they behave. I just wanted you to know that you're family, always have been. Claire and I will continue on as we have, but ..."

Ian could see that Dan was having trouble with this. Ian too was having a hard time. He nodded. He said to Dan, "I know Mary and ... well I know everyone here means a lot to you."

Dan said, "Well I want to see all of this construction completed around here. It'll take a couple of years till everything settles back down. Katie's growing so fast. Soon she'll have a brother ..."

Ian laughed, "Yeah their family's getting bigger."

Dan said, "I just wanted to say something to you about it, that's all. We're going to have some paperwork drawn up – just in case anything were to happen to us. That way ..."

Ian cut him off, "Nonsense, nothing's going to happen. No more trees are going to fall on you Dan, or Claire either for that matter."

Dan laughed, "Maybe not, but we'll still take care of this. Besides, I may have another project coming up in the next couple of years that'll keep me occupied!"

Ian gave him a questioning look, imploring him for more information.

Dan smiled, "Too early to elaborate, I'll get back to you with the details when things start to gel."

May 2, 1863

afternoon

Lieutenant Hawkins and Sergeant Carson were riding hard once again. They were across the Rappahannock and Rapidan rivers, approaching Chancellorsville from the northwest. They had been ordered to circle out far to the west and make sure the Confederate forces left flank wasn't flanking the Union right - while the Union left was attempting to push past the Confederate right as part of a double envelopment – to attack Lee from two directions. As Henry had said to Dewey, 'If war weren't so terrible, it would be laughable.' The two had become a lot closer in the past year. The struggles they had faced at Harpers Ferry and Shepherdstown in the aftermath of Antietam, had truly forged a lifetime friendship. Although neither would admit to the friendship - they had both learned it was easier to not have 'friends' than to make friendships only to see them disappear in a cloud of gunpowder and blood.

The two had dismounted and moved into the woods to look things over. As they moved through the woods, side by side, Dewey said to Henry, "Henry, do you think we'll ever live normal lives after the war?"

Henry had to smile at Dewey, "What makes you think we'll survive?"

Dewey often thought the same thing, although he never said anything about it. "All I'm saying Henry, is that a normal life seems so far away now. It seems like I was a kid then, not knowing too much about what I wanted to do with my life. And look at me now. All I know about, is killing. Same with you if you don't mind me saying it."

    Henry nodded, he couldn't argue with Dewey. He had tried to push all thoughts about his previous life to the back of his mind. As he told Dewey on more than one or two occasions, 'The more you think about the past, or your future life, the sooner your current one will end.' But he did think about Sycamore Glen from time to time and wondered how he would fit back in after the war. After more than two years he had not heard any news from anyone there. When he'd left, he hadn't received any promises from anyone. As far as he knew they probably hadn't given him much more thought. His biggest concern was Jack. Henry knew that Ezekiel would take care of Jack, as long as Jack could work. So, assuming Jack listened to Ezekiel at least 'some' of the time, Jack would do fine. Jack had shown a liking for Sarah, maybe because Jack could sense that Henry liked Sarah. So, Henry hadn't really dwelled on Sycamore Glen very often. He had sent a couple of letters to Sarah in the first few months after he'd left, but they had never been answered. She had probably moved on with her life. Maybe her father had been right. Maybe she had married Josiah after all.

    Henry only nodded and said to Dewey, "Yeah kid, we've gotten pretty good at it, haven't we?" He continued on, not directly talking to Dewey, but just saying what Dewey was probably thinking, "Other men line up shoulder to shoulder and move forward into battle when ordered, while those around them are torn apart, becoming just so much debris. But we quietly stalk those that we think will make a bigger difference ...in the same outcome."

    Up ahead of them, there was movement. They stopped immediately. Both men moved to the muzzles of their horses not wanting any sound to give away their position. The troops approaching, were not coming from the south, but the west. The Union troops were being flanked. Henry turned his horse back north and with Dewey following closely, they carefully moved back the way they came. They would have to move fast. If they didn't, this would turn into a disaster. Maybe they were already too late.

May 2, 1863

late evening

Henry and Dewey had returned with the news, but it was too late. Jackson had gotten around the Union flank. He was pummeling the XI corps. The Union was retreating, trying to regroup and prevent a full-blown catastrophe. Henry and Dewey were back out beyond the flank now, to do what they could, to watch for an even greater flanking movement. They were close in to the Confederate pickets. The danger now was that the troops under Jackson were moving towards Mead's troops on the right flank. If they pushed Meade back and captured the U.S. Ford across the Rappahannock river, the Union forces would be trapped between Lee and Jackson, with their backs against the Rappahannock, and would be crushed before help arrived from Sedgwick who was at Fredericksburg. Hooker's well laid plan was falling apart.

There was sporadic rifle fire throughout the evening as they lay there quietly. Then, they could hear hoof beats, a small group of riders was making its way through the thick growth along a very narrow roadway that Henry had spotted. It wasn't much more than the deer runs that Henry had hunted along as a teenager. Being quiet and patient was what is was all about then – and now.

The small group of riders pulled up to talk quietly. Henry softly nudged Dewey, this was it. Just as Henry began pulling back on the trigger, and his shot rang out, the rebel sentries fired a volley, as did Dewey a moment later. The nearby pickets fired another volley. Several riders went to the ground, others remained in their saddles. Horses from those on the ground galloped back the way they'd come from – back toward the Union lines. There was more gunfire from the pickets, but Henry and Dewey had only fired once, each. Someone in the group was screaming for the firing to stop. They waited for several minutes before moving back to where they'd tied the horses, much closer to the stream that they had crossed and re crossed several times during the evening.

As they retreated towards their camp Dewey asked Henry, "Did you get your man? I think I hit mine."

Henry looked across at Dewey, "Yes, I hit him, he had a raincoat on. Must have been somebody important. If I didn't, then one of his own idiot pickets did, he was hurt. A bunch of them were carrying him back towards their lines."

The next day Henry and Dewey learned from their Captain that Stonewall Jackson had been wounded. A prisoner had said he heard that the wound was serious enough for J.E.B Stewart to take command of Jackson's men before he, in turn, was also wounded. The Captain said to them, "Say, isn't that where you two were last night? Was that your work?" he said to Henry.

Henry looked at Dewey then the Captain, "No sir, I don't think so. We fired on a small party that was out past the pickets, but I think the pickets did the damage. The light back in those trees wasn't that good. You know how it is when everybody starts firing – chaos."

The Captain looked at them, he didn't believe this story for a second. "Well whoever shot Jackson deserves a medal for getting him off the battlefield, even if it is only for a couple of days."

Henry was watching Dewey. He'd let Dewey know by his look that he'd handle this conversation. Henry said, "Well sir, I think you'd have to pass through the lines to pin that medal on some poor bastards' chest from the south. Can you imagine how he must feel – shooting Jackson? I'd rather have all those boys over there take it out on him, rather than on Sergeant Carson here, and myself. Wouldn't you agree Sergeant Carson?"

Dewey smiled at the Captain, nodded in agreement with Henry and said, "Yes sir, it's like Lieutenant Hawkins said sir. It was dark out there, and a lot of people were firing."

The Captain nodded in agreement, smiling at the two of them. "Well as you say, it was dark out there – even for a full moon – wasn't it?"

~ *May 15, 1863* ~

Finally, we've received word about Henry. There was a newspaper article about the fighting in northern Virginia near a place called Chancellorsville. The article mentioned that a Lieutenant Henry Hawkins had been involved in heavy fighting. The article was vague about his actions. It appeared that the article was just mentioning as many men as possible from Henry's unit that had been heavily involved in trying to prevent the rebels from overrunning the Union forces.

~ 31 ~

The guests for the party at Johnny's had almost filled the restaurant. Nancy had insisted they close it from the public against Teddy and Mavis' wishes. But Nancy knew that it would be filled anyway. Teddy and Mavis had a lot of close friends. Some of Barbara's friends from college and several others from Jasper that hadn't moved away were glad for the opportunity to catch up with her. Their lives were all so busy, life seemed to be rushing by so fast.

Davis Templeton was also at the party. In the last several weeks he and Barbara had started dating after they seemed to run into each other more and more frequently. Barbara knew it was no accident, she liked Davis, they had fun together. She wondered how much trouble he had gone through to 'accidentally' cross paths with her so often.

The meals served were a variety of what Johnny's was known for. As Teddy looked around the table, he could see that most people had made it through their meals. There were ten different conversations going on when Teddy stood to speak. He didn't need to tap his glass, when Teddy looked as though he had something to say, people listened.

"Mavis and I want to thank everyone for making it here tonight, we just wanted you to have a chance to say hi to Barbara before she was off again." He said this while smiling at Barbara. "I know that the next semester is a 'ways off but, …" He looked at Barbara as she stood up.

"What my father is trying to say is that I won't be here much longer." As Barbara said this, the room completely quieted down as everyone focused on her.

"When I came home at the break, I told my mom and dad that I was going to do something a little different during the break. They listened, and I think I've convinced them this is right for me."

Heads were turning to look at Mavis and Teddy. They were smiling, waiting for Barbara to continue.

"Next week I'll be leaving for some training that will last from eight to twelve weeks. Then I'll be posted to an overseas unit with the Peace Corps."

There were still some smiles around the table as everyone seemed to wait for a moment or two for a cue from Teddy. Mavis jumped in, "Barb we're so proud of you." At that, the floodgates opened as everyone tried congratulating her at once. Teddy was beaming. Dan slapped him on the back, genuinely happy for him.

Susan was sitting beside Barbara and rose to give her a hug before Barbara sat back down. Davis was sitting on the other side of Barbara and he tried to look at least a little excited for Barbara.

Barbara began facing a barrage of questions as others gravitated towards her. Dan just looked at Teddy and said, "Life.", as he pushed back from the table a little to move aside as others came in close to talk with Mavis and Teddy. Russell and Nancy were at the far end of the table and motioned for Dan to join them. As he made his way to them, Claire joined him.

Russell said to him, "Let's sit over here and give them some room." He motioned to an empty booth. The four of them sat as the questions swirling around Barbara made it impossible to hear each other.

Claire said to Nancy, "A big adventure is just starting over there."

Nancy laughed. "Mavis and Teddy seem to be handling this pretty well."

Russell said to Dan, "It's hard to see them go."

Nancy put her hand on Russell's.

Claire said, "How is Patricia and her husband, since we're talking about children?"

Russell was beaming as he said, "She's fine. So is Steven. I wish they lived closer though."

Nancy was watching Russell closely. She turned to Claire and quietly said, "So, are you and Dan still thinking of adopting, if you don't mind me asking?"

Dan was smiling, Claire said, "Oh yes we're thinking about it. But we're so much older than most of the others that are adopting."

"Nonsense.", said Russell. "Look at us. We were an 'older' couple when we adopted Patricia. Everything worked out fine."

Nancy refocused on Russell, Russell looked at Nancy, she nodded almost imperceptibly. He returned the nod. "Dan why don't you follow me into the wine cellar. I've got some brandy I keep for special occasions. This seems like one. We'll let the ladies discuss this further."

Dan smiled at Claire as he stood to follow Russell.

Russell led Dan through to the kitchen and downstairs into the cellar. There was an impressive rack of bottles against the back wall. He had a small table with several chairs for occasions like this when he'd invite a close friend down to sample a wine and maybe have a quick meal away from the bustling restaurant.

As Dan sat, Russell gathered up two glasses from a cabinet and moved to the rack. He located the bottle he was after and settled down at the table with Dan. He broke the seal of the bottle and extracted the cork with a screw that lay on the table. He poured a sample into a glass and moved it in front of Dan. Dan sipped it and smiled. Russell poured Dan a full glass then filled his.

Dan said to him, "I haven't tasted anything like this in a while. Good."

Russell said, "This is special. It's from my home, Olmobello."

Dan nodded his head – he knew the region. "The hills there are much like the hills here."

Russell continued, "I come from a long line of vintners." He took a sip of his wine.

Dan remained silent.

"I still have relatives there." Added Russell. "This isn't the same as our families', but it's close."

Dan said, "I remember the vines on the hillsides – most were destroyed."

Russell smiled knowingly. He liked Dan. He said to him, "You and I have much in common."

Dan said to him, "I suppose we do. We've both been around. Seen a lot."

Russell said to him, "Too much, at times I suppose."

Dan looked at Russell, a knowing look passed between them.

Dan said to him, "You too then?"

Russell nodded, "Not by choice, but yes. You?"

Dan said, "I enlisted, felt I had to."

Russell said to Dan, "Well, Nancy has spoken to Claire a little. She doesn't say much, it's hard for her. Not very easy for me either."

Dan said, "Oh I know. Claire's told me a little, she's not one to pry, but I know."

Russell said to him, "So you came ashore at Anzio?"

Dan nodded.

Russell said, "I too, was at Anzio. The fascists came for me not long before that. They told me I had to come with them and fight the Americans. I wanted no part of the war, or the fascists. They gave me a choice, one had a knife. Nancy was there …"

Dan was quiet. Nodding his head in an understanding gesture.

"So, I went to fight. During the fighting, I fired over the heads of those coming ashore. I threw some grenades but never pulled the pins. We retreated. I found the soldier with the knife and made sure he wouldn't come for anyone else in the night to fight with the fascists. The unit I was with was almost destroyed, so I left that part of the war. I joined the resistance - to fight the fascists."

Dan continued listening.

"When I first came to them, they said 'We have no weapons for you to fight with. But we will soon get more.' I said to them, 'Don't worry, I bring my own weapon.', and I show them this …", at which point Russell reached down towards his ankle and retrieved a small knife in a sheath. He sat it on the table in front of Dan. The knife handle had the word "Gionata" carved into it.

Dan studied the knife. Russell motioned that he should pick it up. As Dan partially removed it from the sheath, Russell said, "It is small …but sharp. It served me well. They offered me other weapons, but I tell them - 'This is all I need. When I fight the war, I want to see the look in each man's face as I take his life.' ."

Dan slid the knife back into the scabbard.

Russell continued, "Later, I helped with translations and was offered the possibility of coming to America. So, we came here to make our life. You honor us by being here, you and Claire are family."

Dan remained quiet, but lifted his glass and quietly said, "Anzio", and smiled as did Russell. Together they drank.

~ 32 ~

Ian was at the bar in MacGregor's the next morning doing his crossword puzzle when Cletus came in for breakfast. Cletus had already worked several hours but had gotten into the habit of having a breakfast with Mary after she arrived for work. They would have coffee while Katie ate her breakfast, then Mary would drive her to school. Katie was enjoying the summer school. And their lives had settled comfortably into the new routine of living up on Sycamore Hill.

Ian looked up at Cletus. "How long did you two stay last night?"

As Cletus settled into a seat at the bar he said, "Morning Dad. We left right after you did. Mary needs her rest. Me too, for that matter. I don't know where Katie gets all the energy."

The kitchen door burst open and Mary came through with her breakfast plate and sat next to Cletus. "Hi there." She said to Cletus. "You left early this morning."

"Sorry I woke you when I left. I tried to be quiet." He said with a guilty look on face.

"Don't worry, I wasn't sleeping." She said. "You were quiet. Katie never woke up either."

"Well I knew I had a full day ahead of me. I know some of the kids we're bringing on for the summer, will be here eager to start their summer jobs."

Ian chuckled. Every season started out like his. All the spring work would drift into summer. And before long they'd be playing catch up. The weather wouldn't fully cooperate …things just never changed.

"Susan will be in later." Mary said. "She knew it would probably be a late night for her, so I told her to come in at noon. She's going to miss Barbara when she leaves for the Peace Corps. I hope they get a chance to spend some time together in the next couple of weeks."

~

Right now, Susan was spending some time together with Chip …in his bed. The two of them had stayed at Johnnies, along with Barbara and Davis, long after everyone else had left. Most had jobs to wake up for in the morning. After their well-guarded secret had been found out, they could be seen around the clubhouse without the guilty feelings that had first inhibited their budding romance.

They tried to keep their time together in line with what was expected of them as employees. Neither wanted to put the other in a compromising situation regarding their jobs.

Since Chip lived in the basement of the Mill, his apartment was usually where Susan could be found, but no one took this for granted. She was not a child. Everyone respected her. Everyone also liked Chip and realized the two were meant for each other.

If you thought only Cletus and Mary had found true love at Sycamore Glen, you'd be wrong.

Chip was a little older than Susan – but not that much older. They had many of the same likes and dislikes of their generation. Rock and Roll music, and the opposite sex were two of the things that had brought them together. While Chip had stayed away from college to become a cabinetmaker, Susan too had decided to not go to college – at least not right away. Teddy and Mavis had tried to steer her onto a path that led to college, but she just didn't think that was right for her.

As close as she and Barbara were, she needed a little space of her own. She tended to be a bit more practical and down to earth, while Barbara was more of a dreamer. The bigger social issues gripping America drew more of Barbara's attention, than her own.

When Chip had been hired, she came to know his steady, deliberate work ethic early on. He was a hard worker who seemed to get along with everyone else at Sycamore Glen. He wasn't a flirt, but always took the time to ask her how her day was going. After a fashion, his break at lunchtime seemed to always coincide with hers and he'd join her to share their lunches. Soon the small talk grew into more meaningful conversions about things they both cared about. He was sharing more of the history of the mill with Susan as he read through the old paperwork he was uncovering in the old mill office.

This morning they had woken up in each other's arms. They had closed Johnnies with Barbara and Davis, then stopped off at Davis' apartment to continue the evening even further. Both were exhausted when they'd finally arrived back at Chip's apartment and they had quickly fallen asleep. But they had woken up not much past the normal time that started their workdays. It took several minutes for them to realize there was no rush to get ready for work. While Chip had gotten up to start a pot of coffee, Susan had stayed in bed. When Chip finally came back into the bedroom with their coffees, Susan was out of bed at the window that looked out over the small pool downstream of the mill wheel. The weather had begun to turn warm, Chips apartment was pleasantly warm now that the massive stonework that was the basis for the mill had been exposed to the warm summer sun over the past month.

She stood nude at the window. Chip had to catch his breath as she turned towards him. The early morning sun was reflecting off the pool and throwing splotches of sunlight across her body as she stood there. The window was tucked back in close to the earthen embankment as the ground around the mill fell off, down towards the basement level of the building. The dazzling display of light was mesmerizing as the patches danced across the curves of her body.

She had the golden glow of a natural blonde-haired girl who spent time in the sun. Her shoulder length hair looked like it took care of itself. She wore almost no makeup – there was no need to. It would only detract from her natural beauty.

~ 33 ~

The planning for the 4th of July celebration had taken everything into consideration. If the weather wouldn't cooperate, they had tents set up, so at least some of the people might stay dry. If the weather turned unusually hot, they had fans set up in the tents, so most everyone would be in the shade and the fans might keep some of the people cool. If the weather was unusually cold, they had heaters set up in the tents, so most everyone would be out of the wind and the heaters might keep some of the people warm.

Essentially it came down to having tents set up.

Claire had finished reading the diary and felt she had a better understanding of Henry Hawkins. As she'd read along, she had discussed all of it with Dan and most of it with her father, but had stayed quiet about it with everyone else. She was disturbed at how the diary ended. Something wasn't right. She couldn't put her finger on it, but … it didn't make sense. When someone would ask her about it, she would cryptically reply with something like, 'I'm getting a sense of what Jasper was like back then, as well as some of the people.'

It's not that she was hiding anything. The more she read, the more she questioned herself about what she'd previously read. Just when she thought she had something figured out, another passage would cause her to stop and back away from reading the diary. This wasn't like a novel that had a beginning, a middle, and an end. It was about real people. Some were her ancestors, almost everyone mentioned was related in some way or another to someone currently living in Jasper.

July 2, 1863

Henry and Dewey were positioned out past the right flank of the Union forces on what was known locally as Culp's Hill. One of several small hills surrounding the village of Gettysburg, Pennsylvania. The land was formed into a small 'saddle' in front of them that led to a small rise just south of the main hill. A stream ran through the low area. This position let them look out beyond the extreme right of the Union line that had formed after the initial fighting that had occurred the day before. Union forces had retreated to a small ridge known as Cemetery Ridge. During the night, the men had dug in and piled up rocks to form a defensive line.. Culp's Hill was located near the north end of the ridge, just outside the village.

"Lieutenant, please have some of your men move out beyond us just a little more. Although, we don't want them too exposed. These woods are good cover, they'll be able to fire out as far as the base of that small rise the next time Johnson's men try to come through there."

Dewey had been looking down towards the stream and turned to Henry, "Captain, you should pull back into the trees a little while I reposition the men. This spot is exposed, there's some rocks just behind us that would do you nicely."

Henry smiled and looked at Dewey, "Lieutenant, I'll take that under advisement after the disposition of the men has been seen to."

Dewey said, "I'll return shortly sir. Stay behind cover."

As Dewey headed out towards the scouts, Henry said, "Dewey be careful out there, we'll have a hell of a day ahead of us tomorrow, not that today was any picnic."

Henry and Dewey hadn't received any medals after the Wilderness debacle. There was a reluctance to award anything to anybody, considering how close the army had come to an all-out collapse. Although they had 'lost' the battle, Lee had lost Jackson. The Union had recovered and was now hot after Lee. In their Division, it did not go unnoticed that Henry and Dewey had probably played a very large role in preventing the collapse. They had received field promotions and their responsibilities increased to include overseeing the scouting activity for the Division. Henry and Dewey were in the process of turning the scouts with good marksmanship skills into exceptional shots. Henry's subtle training techniques with Dewey, had been absorbed by others, Dewey was working with several of the men in teams of two, to give the Division a long range, lethal, punch. He had adapted Henrys technique of 'lead shooter - subordinate shooter', to become more of a 'one shooter - one lookout/protector' team. This allowed the designated shooter to get more than one or two shots off at a target without worrying so much about his own safety. Dewey felt that if the 'protector' was not directly alongside the shooter, the enemy would have a larger target area to concern themselves with, perhaps even believing they were under attack by a larger force.

Today, though, everything was about massed firepower. In the earlier attempts to take the hill, it had come down to having a superior position to defend, with partial entrenchments having been hastily constructed during the night. Being able to stay positioned behind the jumble of rocks strewn about the hill, as well as the thick trees, had helped save lives. No one knew how many more charges the rebels would attempt, but they hadn't pulled back much, and they were sure to resume the assault sometime the next day.

July 3, 1863

The sun had not yet come up when the Union artillery opened fire on the rebels. This preceded an attack against the rebels by elements of the I and XII Corps that were defending Culp's Hill. After nearly seven hours of fighting, the battle for Culp's Hill was over - the Union had held the position. This was some of the longest sustained fighting, not just at Gettysburg, but at any time during the war. The rebels had pulled away, their retreat would go largely unanswered. To those that thought there should have been an aggressive pursuit of Lee, the defenders of Culp's Hill would probably have had cause to argue. They were dog tired, hungry, shot up and generally near the end of their rope. The movement of troops about the field of battle, where they had been needed most, coupled with fresh troops who had not yet faced the enemy - had been brilliant.

Amidst this devastated landscape, units were reforming, trying to treat the wounded and awaiting further orders. Henry had taken Dewey's advice - it had probably saved his life. He had nearly a dozen bullet tears in his uniform, but none had apparently drawn blood. Not many were as lucky as him. His junior officers were seeing to their men, several had reported the extent of the deaths and injuries their details had sustained. Dewey had not shown up yet, Henry was becoming concerned. Dewey had positioned his men directly in front of a force pushing forward more successfully than some of the other troops that had come at them. Finally, Dewey came up to Henry to report in. As Dewey saluted, Henry could see his arm tied off with a makeshift bandage. He had somewhat gingerly hobbled up to Henry to make his report. Henry told him to sit as he returned the salute. He helped Dewey down onto a nearby stone.

Dewey was looking for the words …" It was bad sir," he began, "Thank god for Christian Sharps," he said as he patted his rifle. "We lost eleven dead and another 17 wounded. Sergeant Stiles …was in the middle of it." Dewey just shook his head, no words to describe how he felt about his Sergeant.

Before he continued, Henry said "You stay seated, I don't want you moving around. We'll be getting some help here to see to the wounded. I'll get everyone rounded up. No orders have come down about any kind of counterattack or pursuit, but they'd be crazy not to try and take advantage of the enemies' retreat."

Dewey carefully stood, and quietly said, "Henry, this is just a scratch," as he indicated the bandage. "I twisted my ankle down there in that muck along the stream, it'll be okay, I can walk on it."

Henry was doubtful and said so. "Dewey, stay on a horse as soon as we get ourselves back together here. I don't want you walking anywhere - understood - Lieutenant?", he added with a smile.

Dewey returned the smile, "We'll see sir, if there are enough horses, I may just ride for a while."

While they were talking, their Colonel came up, "Gentlemen, fine work out there, until I can get with everyone, make sure everybody knows that. It could have gone against us in a bad way, but thanks to them …" he motioned down towards the stream at the troopers, "it didn't. Damn fine men." He too, couldn't say much more, drained from being able to express himself any better than that. "Lieutenant Carson …you and your men were …exceptional out there. Henry, you held this end of the line …I thought they'd turned us …magnificent …really."

He looked at Henry's uniform, almost at a loss for words. "Henry, you need a new uniform.", he said nodding towards Henry's sleeve that had three holes in it that he could see. When you get it, make sure some oak leaves are sewn on. I don't want anyone mistaking you for a Captain anymore."

Henry tried to speak, but the Colonel cut him short by waving it off. He added, "Make sure you cut the bars off this uniform carefully. Captain Carson here, should look presentable with them sewn on his new uniform. Don't you think?"

Henry smiled and nodded in agreement.

Dewey just nodded a tired 'Thank you', stood, and saluted the Colonel. The Colonel returned the salute, said a quiet 'Thank you son.', patted his shoulder and moved away. He was studying some of the wounded, slowly making their way back to them, having been replaced in the line by others that had not been directly engaged yet. He shook his head and walked back towards another cluster of his officers in the process of reforming their troopers.

~ *July 4, 1863* ~

I thought of trying to write to Henry but don't know if I should. I'm sure he had his reasons for not writing after he left. I can't imagine what he must be going through. We're receiving news by the telegraph of a very large battle happening somewhere in Pennsylvania. I pray that Henry is okay. They say they will be posting casualty lists after the fighting is over.

No one said the war would last this long ...

~ 34 ~

When Claire's turn came to speak, she was fine. She had long ago learned how to keep the nervousness out of her voice when addressing an audience. She had heard of many tricks speakers used. Her delivery wasn't based on trickery, it was based on knowing the material she was speaking about, so thoroughly, that she usually felt she was short changing her audience with the subset of material she had spoken about, as opposed to the greater volume she was prepared to speak about.

Today's speech was no different. She had written everything out – several times – so she was comfortable with the facts she was presenting. Getting the rhythm of the phrases set in a comfortable pattern to help her speak in a conversational tone, not merely reciting facts. Several of the top-rated papers that the students had written had already been presented. These were gifted students, passionate about what they had learned about the Civil War. Claire's plan was to stay focused on Henry Hawkins. She had learned much more about Henry as she read through the diary and had asked around town, visiting family members of some of the families whose names she'd encountered in the diary. Most everyone had tidbits of family history that had been handed down over the years, they were more than willing to share them with Claire.

She began by mentioning that what was in the 'time capsule' would be on display in the library until the capsule was resealed later in the summer.

"As you all know we've unsealed the time capsule and what we found inside has been catalogued and mentioned in several news articles written over the last couple of months. We've decided to hold off resealing everything until later in the year. This gives everyone a chance to look at the display in the library. It also gives us a little time to transcribe an item in the capsule that was a complete surprise to us. The item is a Hawkins family diary. I've been reading through it since we unsealed the vault for Henry Hawkins here at the monument back in April." There was a little chatter amongst the people gathered to hear the mayor speak.

She continued, "The material in the diary is quite revealing. It's not just about the Hawkins family, but to a large degree is about Jasper and the farming community that was, and still is, centered in Jasper. There's also a good deal of information about how the mill in Sycamore Glen operated."

"What we plan on doing is keeping the actual diary within the family for further study, but, placing a complete copy back in the capsule using a more stable material than what is was originally written on. I know the materials that the students used are very stable and should last easily another fifty or seventy-five years without any deterioration."

"As a descendant of Henry Hawkins, in a manner of speaking, I've been almost mesmerized by the picture of him that has come forward after reading the diary. Most of you know that my father, Judge Osborn, is the grandson of Henry Hawkins. This isn't exactly the case. Henry was the second husband of the Judge's grandmother. Her first husband, Jedidiah Prescott, died at the very start of the war, never knowing he had a daughter. Henry married Ruth Jennings Prescott when he returned home from the war, and helped Ruth raise her daughter, Clarissa, as if she were his own daughter.

The one aspect of Henry's character that has become clear is that he did not think of himself as a hero. I think it's easy for us to think of him as heroic, given what we know about the Civil War and the ferocity of the fighting that he must have experienced. But he never expressed his wartime experiences in that manner. He entered the war as a private in the infantry, but steadily rose through the ranks based on his performance, and later, his leadership skills. During the war, his actions and very existence went largely unknown to our community. It must be presumed that the flow of information about him, from the battlefield, to his home here in Jasper, just never really came about. This may have been due in large part to Henry's reluctance to stay in touch with anyone here. After the war, he admitted that during much of the time, he didn't think about the future, he tried to stay focused on the war – to stay alive. I think this attitude helped keep others alive that were under his command. So, although he may not have thought of himself as a 'hero', I'd like to believe that by his actions, by the very nature of his being, he was a hero. There are references in the diary that mention visitors Henry had, many years after the war, that sought him out to specifically thank him for keeping them alive.

There is also a passage in the diary that mentions his displeasure at the thought of a statue being erected in his honor. I think he was pleased that this didn't happen – at least while he was alive. This monument was erected fifty years after the battle of Gettysburg. I'm sure most of you have seen the names of the other battles that Henry Hawkins fought in that encircle the base of the monument. These are all familiar names to everyone. We'll never know precisely what his involvement was in all of them. I think what's important for us to remember is that he did his duty when asked to, that his actions, like many others that fought in the war, helped preserve the union, guaranteeing the movement forward of our society, our current freedoms, our very existence."

With her remarks finished, there was a warm round of applause from the audience. Most were older residents. With so many activities taking place around the town, Claire was surprised to see so many people at the monument. Many were parents of the students that had read their material that was going to be included in the capsule when it was resealed. Prominent in the front row were Dan and Claire's father.

The Judge looked every bit the proud father as Claire spoke. She had inherited some of the same qualities that the judge possessed in speaking to a large gathering. While she had spoken, it was apparent that the judge was in attendance. Everyone from Jasper and the immediate vicinity knew the Judge on sight. But even those who had never met him would not have had a problem identifying him as he stood when Claire exited the podium and the crowd began to disperse.

One such person was a dapper looking, white haired gentleman who approached Claire as she stood next to Dan and the Judge. "Madam, I want to thank you for your lovely remarks concerning Mr. Hawkins, and by extension, others that fought in the war. If I may introduce myself, I'm Peter Fisher – my mother was Sally Carson, daughter of Andrew and Carlotta Carson. If you've been studying material about Mr. Hawkins, you may know of my grandfather as - Dewey."

~ 35 ~

Peter Fisher was warmly greeted by the Judge. After shaking hands with everyone as the Judge introduced him to the circle of friends from town and the golf course that been seated near him, he drew Peter off to the side to sit and learn more about his family. About each other really, Peter had as many questions concerning Henry and his descendants as the Judge had about Dewey.

It was getting later in the afternoon when Dan and Claire suggested that the small group still chatting with them come across the square to their house where they'd be more comfortable, and they could have a meal. Claire had prepared enough food, expecting their friends would want to stay together beyond the ceremony – later into the pleasant mid-summer evening.

Peter was staying at a hotel just outside town near the interstate and couldn't be persuaded to stay with Dan and Claire. He didn't want to be an imposition on anyone. But he wasn't in a rush to leave. He would stay over for a couple days – long enough to see all of Jasper and make a trip up to the golf course and perhaps visit Mary and Cletus at their home.

May 2, 1864

Major Hawkins and Captain Carson had worked hard with their sharpshooters. During the winter encampment, each sharpshooter spent time with Henry and Dewey to hone their skills. This wasn't just about the mechanics of shooting - Henry wanted each man to be tougher mentally. He knew that each man he was working with, would be considered an exceptional marksman by others, but that wasn't good enough for Henry.

He had watched one young man put shot after shot into a target at three hundred yards. The target was a silhouette target – Henry disliked the silhouettes. He came up behind the man to compliment him on his accuracy. "Looks like you've got a good pattern there, all in the head." He said nodding down the range that had been set up.

"Thank you, sir." The man replied as he reloaded his Sharps rifle.

Henry said to him, "Hold off a moment, I want to chat with you a bit."

"Of course, sir." The main responded.

Henry smiled, "Stand easy son, you're not doing anything wrong. I just wanted give you something to think about, that's all."

The young soldier relaxed a little.

Henry looked at him, "You see Captain Carson down there a 'ways?"

The man replied, "Yes sir."

Henry said, "Take a look at his target."

The soldier looked downrange, adjusting his eyesight to try to see it more clearly. Henry handed him his field glasses, "Here, try these."

The man put them up to his face, slightly adjusting them.

"What do you see for his pattern down there?" Asked Henry.

"Well sir, it is a tight pattern, a very tight pattern. Center of the chest." He handed the glasses back to Henry.

Henry said, "The thing is, Captain Carson and I have learned that when you're trying to hit a target, and all hell is breaking loose around you, a bigger target is better."

The man stayed quiet, sensing Henry had more to add.

"You're a fine shot, son. I probably can't teach you much more to improve on that. But what I can help you with, is the process of killing someone or taking him out of the war." Henry motioned him back from the firing line, to sit with him.

Henry said, "Sorry, but I've forgotten your name …"

The corporal helped him out, "It's Hutchinson sir, Robert Hutchinson."

The two sat, Henry continued, "Well Bob, this is not about trying to just shoot someone, it's about preventing an officer in charge of a large number of men from doing his job. I don't want you to shoot some poor private or corporal that is out there opposite you, occasionally sending a round in your direction. We won't end the war that way. I want you looking for that man out there who seems to be in charge. He may be on a horse, maybe not. He may be an enlisted man. Some sergeants I've met are twice as effective as a leader than some officers I've seen in action. Use your eyes to find that person and eliminate him."

The man was thinking this over.

Henry continued, "I've seen the effect of an officer going down, on the men around him, on other officers. It's devastating. It creates chaos, disorganization. That's what we want."

Dewey had come over to see what the conversation was all about. As he listened to Henry, he could see the young man absorbing this.

Henry said, "Captain Carson, have you ever had occasion to shoot a horse?"

Dewey answered, "Yes sir, on several occasions."

Henry continued, "And why sir, was that necessary?"

Dewey responded, "Well sir, it was somewhat chaotic trying to lock in on the officer, so I figured I could at least unhorse him, maybe kill him that way."

Henry asked, "Did it work?"

"Yes sir." Dewey answered, "I didn't see him get up, at least not right away. I was busy finding other targets."

Henry smiled, he knew what Dewey's answer would be. They'd had this conversation in front of other shooters. It was true. Do what you could, to take the man out of the war.

Dewey added, "That's why I always practice hitting the chest of my target. I don't want to risk not taking him out of action by shooting his ear off or putting a round through his cheek. If I'm off a little with a chest shot, he may not be killed outright, but he's not going to be fighting anymore anytime soon."

Henry agreed, "The other thing is that by shooting that much lower, even if he missed, he might still hit someone else. I see too many men shooting high, missing everything."

"A final question Captain," said Henry. "Do you know the color of the horse that Robert Lee rides?"

"Which one sir?" answered Dewey. "I know for a fact that he has three horses he's been seen riding. Possibly a fourth."

Henry said, "His favorite – any idea?"

"Yes sir." Answered Dewey. "A large stallion, gray with a dark mane and tail, he calls him Traveller. I've always got an eye open for him."

Henry said, "You see son, Captain Carson is a hunter. He knows all about his prey. He's always learning. That's what I want from you. Keep on learning. Use the habits of your enemy to your advantage. He's going to keep trying to kill you. Be better."

Dewey nodded in agreement and walked back to where he had been shooting, leaving Henry with his student.

Henry continued, "I'm teaching you to be not just a hunter, but a skilled killer. You're up against a very dangerous adversary. He may be as good a shot as you. I need you to use everything to your advantage to kill your target and survive to kill another."

Henry stood, signaling the man to go back to his practice.

As the man stood he said, "Thank you sir, I'll try to remember all this."

"Well", Henry said, "keep practicing, think of the target out there as someone shooting back at you. Survive."

Henry walked down to where Dewey was practicing. As he came up behind him, Dewey ceased firing and joined Henry back from the others practicing. Quietly Henry said to him, "Dewey, best wrap things up here. We're going to be moving out tomorrow. They want us south, back towards Chancellorsville."

Dewey nodded, "I thought we'd be on the move before too much longer. That's good, everybody is itchy to do something. We'll get a chance to see what these boys here have learned."

Henry agreed but added, "I just remember what a mess it was in there last year. Either you're marching down a road in plain view or you're trampling through that snarled up mess of a woods not being able to see anything."

May 5, 1864

afternoon

Dewey had taken corporal Hutchinson and had gotten out on the flank, ahead of the rest of the division. They had been riding carefully along the Orange Plank road, ducking in and out of the woods alongside the road. They had been off the roadway for a while when they spotted an opening in the woods that looked out into a large meadow. They tied their horses and carefully ventured forward, to look out into the clearing. When they came out of the trees they surprised a group of three or four rebels just across the clearing, not a hundred yards away. Sitting near their horses.

At about the same time, a line of union skirmishers from further back behind them along the road, also began emerging from the woods. The rebels saw them and began moving back into the trees. The two groups were only clearly visible to each other for a few moments. Neither had enough time to initiate any real action, the union skirmishers appeared a little confused about the sudden confrontation. Dewey and Hutchinson had their pistols drawn, but both had instinctively moved back to their horses to retrieve their rifles. As they came back into the opening, the rebels were gone, and the skirmishers were also no longer visible.

Dewey said to Hutchinson, "Did you see those horses?"

"Yes sir." Said Hutchinson. "One of them was gray with a dark mane and tail."

Dewey said, "There's going to be hell to pay for missing this opportunity. It's been reported that Hill and Ewell are up now, and Longstreet can't be far behind either. Some of them must have been conferring with Lee. ... Damn it!

May 6, 1864

At dawn Dewey came to Henry's tent. The campsite had been hurriedly thrown together after the fighting died down the previous evening. Nobody had gotten much sleep. Everyone was on edge, waiting for the fight to resume at daybreak. Most had eaten at least a little, not much - it would have to get them through the day.

Henry looked up as Dewey approached. Dewey saluted, as he always did at the start of a new day. He truly respected Henry, as did Henry of Dewey – he returned the salute. "Morning Dewey." Said Henry quietly, not wishing to wake everyone up just yet.

"Morning sir." Said Dewey softly in response. "Suppose we best get everyone up." He added, more of a question than a statement.

"Yes Dewey, its time. The staff sent a courier down to let me know they want some of us to get out there on the flank. We may be moving further south. Depends on what develops here this morning. We're supposed to see if any flanking movement can be undertaken. In this jungle? Impossible!" He finished with a snort as he waved into the maze of trees and undergrowth.

Dewey turned back toward the trees. It was light enough to make out some of them, but the air was thick with smoke from the fires that had started yesterday. The acrid bitterness of the smoke confirmed the rumors that more than trees and brush had burned. Men from both sides had died in the flames, wounds leaving them unable to move and escape a fiery death. The fighting had been ferocious, but indecisive. Their scouts and sharpshooters had not been as effective as everyone had hoped for. It did little good to specialize in shooting at distances of hundreds of yards when everything blurred into a kaleidoscope of underbrush, tree limbs, smoke, gray clad rebels and blue coated federals at distances of tens of yards.

"Captain, let's get the men up. Take several out beyond our flank. Stay close enough to be able to report on any enemy movement. The rest of us will be moving out behind you shortly. Let's not get too separated from everyone else here, I think we'll be needed when things get hot again."

Dewey saluted, Henry returned it and added, "Be safe out there Dewey, look out for the boys. Keep me informed if anything develops."

"Understood sir. We won't be so far off that we'll have any trouble getting back to you." Said Dewey as he moved off towards his men. He knew who he'd take with him. He'd seen most in action yesterday, several stood out, a couple others - he wanted to see some more of - before he asked them to go out there on their own. Once they got out of this damnable thicket!

~ 36 ~

Cletus had talked extensively with Peter Fisher and spent more time with the Judge who seemed to have regained some of his old vigor when around the golf course. He hadn't golfed recently, and Peter was no golfer, but together, they both enjoyed the pub.

The three were in the Judges booth talking about the course. The Judge turned to Peter and said, "Have I told you yet, about how I met Cletus here at the course?"

Peter smiled, "Not yet Judge, how'd that come about?"

The Judge said, "Well I know you've been told about Dan bringing him here to the course, but I actually met him out there. I think it was on number 11, wasn't it Cletus?"

Cletus nodded. He had to smile about it now.

The Judge continued, "I sliced a shot off number 17 fairway into the rough by number 11 green. There was a big discussion about me trying to hack it out of there to save a stroke. I failed miserably, but Cletus here, lofted a shot out of that snarled up mess and put it on the green in splendid position."

Peter chuckled and let the Judge continue.

"Then he proceeded to duplicate that remarkable feat with a shot that was even closer, while being the object of some wagering by our two groups of golfers."

Cletus smiled as he said, "Well Judge, as you now know, I wasn't then, and still am not, a golfer."

The Judge said with a twinkle in his eye, "Oh I know. There's many things you are, and I guess a golfer is not one of them." He hesitated, looked around the pub furtively, to see how many people were nearby, and in a quiet voice said, "But I do know something else … something you're not."

Cletus said, "What would that be, Judge?"

The Judge responded, "That business before you came here." He smiled at Cletus, " … Nonsense."

Peter looked at the Judge.

The Judge said, "Cletus led us to believe he had been in some trouble, but ... well, we'll discuss this further at another time. It's probably not best to discuss this with our guest here Cletus.", he said motioning toward Peter.

Cletus smiled at the Judge, 'How did he find out?' He said, "Well I don't care if Peter hears about your 'theory', but it's probably a good idea for us to discuss this another time, I have to get back out there.", he said pointing out towards the course. "Peter, nice seeing you again. I hope you can stay a little longer this time." He reached across to shake Peter's hand as he got up to leave. As he stepped away from the table, he gave the judge a sly smile, winked, and was off to continue his work.

After Cletus had walked away from the table, Peter asked the Judge, "I hope I wasn't preventing you two from discussing something important?"

The Judge said, "No, we'll pick it up later. I just thought it might be time to correct any misconceptions about what might have happened in Cletus' past. I think he's been carrying something around for a while, that ...well, I know a little about carrying a secret around. I think we should end his secret. Probably no need for it anymore, just like mine.".

~ 37 ~

There were more people wandering into the pub as the afternoon wore on. The Judge and Peter were still in the corner booth at MacGregor's enjoying their coffee.

Peter said, "I wanted to ask Cletus about visiting the pond up by his house but forgot to before he left to continue working after lunch."

The Judge said, "Well we can certainly borrow a cart and visit the pond, whenever you'd like."

Peter continued, "Well I remembered about the pond this morning after I got up. My mother had told me a story about the pond when I was quite young. I've been trying to recall her stories about when she visited here as a young girl on her way to school in Philadelphia."

The judge was patient, interested in what came next.

Peter went on, "While she was visiting, there was a big picnic held on the fourth of July up at the pond. She described the setting up there as one of utter beauty. There was a large table set up under a massive Sycamore tree beside the pond. Beneath the tree was a really large mill stone that 'uncle' Henry explained covered the grave of his mule Jack."

The Judge was intently following the story, "'Uncle' Henry he asked?"

Peter explained, "Well apparently your grandfather didn't like to be addressed as 'Mr. Hawkins" by Sally so he suggested 'Uncle'

Henry. As he explained it, Dewey and he were brothers after all they'd been through during the war

October 18, 1864

Henry and Dewey had moved from the 159th Pennsylvania Regiment to the 80th back in the summer. Henry's skills were becoming more widely known and it was agreed that he would move through the Divisions in the VIII Corps to train their sharpshooters. He seemed to bring out that extra 'something' that turned good marksmen into something special, more than what they had been capable of before meeting Henry and Dewey.

Currently they were serving with the 59th (Pennsylvania) Regiment of the 3rd Brigade of the 1st Division of the VIII Corps and were encamped near a small stream just outside Strasburg, Virginia. It was mid-October. The unit had withstood a bombardment of their position the day before. Thinking that their adversary, Jubal Early, was pulling back down the valley turnpike towards New Market, the Union forces had relaxed somewhat and held their position in a line that stretched along the valley turnpike south of Middleton, just north of Strasburg. The right end of the line was anchored against the banks of a small stream called Cedar Creek. The lines ran generally southward somewhat near the creek, then doubled back along the turnpike. Henry's unit was in a more southern position near a depressed area, close to the confluence of the north branch of the Shenandoah river and the meandering end of Cedar Creek.

The pickets were out as everyone gathered about their campfires and ate their evening meal. Henry had seen most of the men shoot and was generally pleased with how they performed. One young man, a corporal Fisher, seemed to possess all the qualities that Henry looked for in a marksman. The trouble was, he was a bit erratic, even though he had already learned most of the skills it took to be really good – even at distances of six hundred yards or more. Henry had filled his plate and motioned to Dewey that they should sit with Fisher.

When they approached, and sat down, Fisher stood and saluted. Henry returned the salute, "Sit down Fisher, please. Relax. Captain Dewey here, and I don't bite. I just wanted to have a word, if you're done eating? May we join you?"

"Certainly sir," stammered Fisher, obviously a little rattled by the sudden appearance of 'the brass'. He was silent as Henry chewed on a mouthful of food.

After Henry swallowed, he continued, "We've been watching you shoot, pretty impressive, wouldn't you say Captain Carson?"

Dewey smiled and nodded; he had seen this technique used before. Henry would put the man at ease and get to the bottom of the problem.

Henry said, "I see that you eat left-handed, but shoot right-handed. How did that come about if you don't mind me asking?"

Fisher was relaxing, after he'd swallowed some coffee he replied, "Well sir, my daddy said that nobody who was left handed would ever amount to anything, so when he taught me to shoot, he taught me right handed. It's the only way I've ever shot."

Dewey smiled and nodded at Henry, then said to Fisher, "You ever try to shoot left-handed - just to see?"

Fisher nodded his head, "Just a couple times, didn't feel right though."

Henry said to him, "Let's try a little something. Grab a small stick."

Fisher reached out and picked up a short stick laying near his feet. "This do?"

Henry nodded yes. "Now hold it out in front of yourself, use both hands if you like. Keep both eyes open and sight on something out there a hundred yards or so using the stick."

Fisher did as he was instructed.

Henry said, "Okay now, don't move your hands - stay steady and close just your right eye."

Fisher obeyed.

Henry continued, "Okay, now open your right eye and close your left eye"

Fisher followed along.

Henry said, "Okay, now that you see what we're doing here, I want you to do this a couple times. First close one eye, then open it and close the other."

Fisher did this also. You could see by his expression that he was seeing something happen in all this.

Henry added, "When you close one of your eyes the object jumps away from the stick doesn't it?"

Fisher was still doing the exercise. "Yes sir, when I close my left eye the tree trunk out there 'jumps' away from the stick.

Henry said, "I thought so, because you're left-handed. Usually someone who is left-handed, like you, has a dominant left eye. This is the eye you should be sighting with – instead, you're closing it and using your weaker eye – the right – sighting down along the barrel. Because that's the way your daddy taught you to shoot. It doesn't always mean it's wrong, but sometimes it can make a difference. Maybe it does with you. The next chance we get we'll try it out. I don't want to make any ruckus tonight by shooting, maybe tomorrow. It might be hard for you to shoot left-handed – at first – but maybe it'll improve your aim, just a little. Sometimes that's all it takes. Worth a try."

Dewey was looking around. Others nearby had overheard and were testing their eyes. He motioned for Henry to look around.

Henry had to chuckle, most of his lessons usually worked out like this. Talking to one soldier helped train everyone nearby. He spoke a little louder so those nearby could hear, "Now, don't everyone here start shooting crosshanded or we'll lose this damn war. Try it when we're practicing, and the shot doesn't matter. Only seen this help a couple people shoot any better. Don't get yourself killed experimenting."

As the discussions lingered on into the evening, a heavy mist rolled into the campsite and the temperature noticeably dropped. They couldn't see the looming heights of Massanutten mountain, the dominant feature at the north end of the Shenandoah valley, any longer. As it grew darker, Henry told everyone not to stay up all night - to get some sleep. Perhaps tomorrow they'd be on the move.

~ 38 ~

Cletus worked up a sweat that afternoon. The Judge's oblique reference to his past had taken him back nearly nine years. After leaving the table in MacGregor's, he'd retrieved his axe from the utility building and made his way up above the number 14 hole and into the woods beyond the green. Separated from everyone, he had begun swinging his axe into a windfall that he'd spotted earlier in the week. He wanted to trim it up somewhat before cutting up the tree to salvage the trunk. He'd be able to saw it up into quite a bit of quality lumber. As the interior work on the clubhouse continued, the plan was to make extensive use of the hardwood Cletus was harvesting from the woods that surrounded the course.

What had led the Judge to make the comment about 'the business' before he'd come to Sycamore Glen? Cletus had pushed it to the back of his mind for years now. He thought it was out of his life. He had explained it all to Mary and Ian. He felt he had to, before he asked Mary to be his wife. The last thing he wanted was to have anyone here involved or affected by what he'd done.

As he continued chopping, he replayed the events that had led him to Sycamore Glen …

As he had explained to Ian and the Judge so long ago, he was devastated when his brother Floyd had been killed in Korea. He attempted to enlist in the Army shortly after that but had been denied based on what he thought was a minor medical condition that had come to light during the enlistment process. What he hadn't discussed with them was that he attempted to work his way around this by approaching a doctor that had been exempting men from the draft based on his diagnosis of non-existent health issues.

Just as he was beginning to put his plan in effect, he was found out. The local authorities were already onto the doctor and convinced Cletus to work with them in putting an end to the doctors' activities. The FBI was involved because of some of the doctors' other activities which Cletus wasn't made aware of initially. He'd agreed to help when they told him there was no way they'd permit him to enlist – because he actually did have a condition that would have put him at risk. They weren't threatening him with any legal action – merely appealing to him to help them. He had met with the doctor on several occasions and the FBI was interested in who else the doctor was involved with – who was that 'somebody higher up' governing the doctors' activities? Cletus agreed to secretly testify before a federal grand jury about what he knew and who else he dealt with besides the doctor.

Things started to fall apart before any legal action could begin. The doctor mysteriously disappeared just before warrants were going to be issued to bring everybody in to face charges of fraudulent activities and conspiracy.

Several weeks later the doctors' body was discovered in a remote wooded area of the county. He was wearing hunting clothes and had been found by other hunters. The problem was that the doctor was not a hunter. It was obviously a poorly executed attempt at disguising the doctors' death as either a hunting accident or suicide.

At the same time, the federal prosecutor spoke with Cletus to let him know that there might have been a leak concerning his secret testimony. They couldn't be sure how much was leaked, but they were almost certain his name had been found out.

What he proposed, was to put Cletus in the federal witness protection program. He explained to Cletus that even though the doctor was dead, there were others involved in the scheme – these were the people they were really after. It might still be possible to use Cletus' testimony when they brought these other criminals into court.

The problem was that they didn't know when that would happen, and they didn't want to risk Cletus' safety in the interim. Cletus had thought through all the ramifications of entering the program. He'd basically disappear. There wouldn't be any contact with anyone. His life wouldn't be his anymore. In the end he decided that he couldn't go through with it.

The prosecutor he was dealing with, was a young energetic attorney that wasn't willing to back away from the case. He didn't want to jeopardize Cletus' life, but he needed to be able to call on him in the future. He was willing to work with Cletus concerning his protection.

Finally, they found a solution. Cletus met with the prosecutor and the federal Judge for the district and he proposed to them that he be found in contempt of court for failing to fully disclose his part in all this. He could then be sent to a local prison by the Judge where he could be guarded. It would be spread around to everyone that it was because of his failure to cooperate that he was being jailed. He'd stay in confinement for a short time until everyone was convinced that he wasn't in danger any longer. This suited Cletus, he wouldn't totally disappear, and when everything worked through the courts he could then decide if he should enter the witness program. He'd also be close to some of the low-level criminals in this scheme and perhaps could gain their confidence to extend his usefulness beyond his initial involvement.

Everyone knew this was somewhat risky, but Cletus convinced the Judge that he could take care of himself in jail.

So off he went for what he thought was a short term but stretched out to almost two years, as events beyond his control played out …

Before long Cletus found himself working on the main trunk of the tree with his axe. He had finally drifted back into the present and stopped cutting after he realized he had cut through the trunk twice with his axe. If he kept this up, all he'd have left from the tree would be a pile of chips.

The sweat was pouring off him, but it felt good. The hot sun and strenuous exercise were almost therapeutic - all other thoughts had melted away as he had continued cutting.

He moved away from the pile of brush, picked up his shirt and began walking back towards the shed where he'd left his cart. He hadn't gotten very far when he came across Mary, headed up the hill from the shed – obviously looking for him.

"There you are.", she said. "I wondered where you had gone off to. Usually you let me know when you're up here by yourself with your axe".

Cletus smiled, "Guess I forgot to call again." He said, remembering back to his 'accident' with his axe on the hill, before they were married – it had happened not too far from where they now stood.

Mary had to laugh but pointed her finger at him in a mock attempt at scolding him.

He took her hand with his free hand and headed them back down the hill out of the woods.

"You still look good without a shirt." Was all she said as they continued back towards their carts near the shed.

~ 39 ~

When they reached their house, Mary led Cletus upstairs to their bathroom. She started the shower, so it would warm up before he jumped in to clean himself up. She watched as he took off the rest of his clothes and got into the shower.

He barely had a chance to soap up before Mary entered the shower. She didn't say a word. She took his washcloth and soaped it up to do his back. When she was finished, she rinsed the cloth out, re soaped it and gave it to Cletus to do her back. As he gently scrubbed her back he encircled her with his free arm to keep her from sliding or falling in the shower.

He was so tender. She enjoyed the feel of his hands on her body. She always had, she always would. As her pregnancy continued, her body had become more sensitive to his touch. He was sliding his hands across her abdomen – it felt good. It wouldn't be much longer before this would have to stop, but for now … it continued.

She said, "You don't have to get back right away, do you?", You can stay for a bit, can't you?"

He smiled, "I can stay for a while."

"Good.", she said as she turned the water off. She reached out onto the vanity and grabbed the two towels laying there. Giving him one, she took the other and began drying herself off. She was drying her hair out as best she could, it wouldn't be completely dry, but it would have to do.

As Cletus finished drying himself, she took his hand and led him out into their bedroom. She led him to the bed and sat with him along the edge of the bed. As they sat there, she lifted his hands to her chest. She knew he wouldn't be able to resist much longer, she enjoyed hurrying him along. Her breasts had enlarged somewhat in the past month or so, and had become quite tender. He'd be careful with her …but she had to feel his hands on her, exploring her …this felt so good.

"Is this why you came looking for me?", he said smiling at her.

"Something like this.", she said.

"You should have come earlier?", he said.

"I haven't come at all,", she said, "… Yet."

"But Mary …", he started to say.

She put her hand up to his lips to silence him.

"Cletus, I need to have you right here, right now. Don't worry, you won't hurt me."

She provided all the movement. She wanted this to last. Neither of them was in a hurry. She moved slowly with purpose, but eventually she couldn't contain herself any longer. When it did happen, everything in her poured out. Her emotions were just beginning to come into play during the pregnancy. Quietly she began crying from the exquisite feelings she was experiencing, Cletus tried to pull away.

As she felt this happening, she pulled him back tighter against her.

"No." she said. "Come closer, don't leave me. Not yet." 'Not ever', she thought.

October 19, 1864

Henry was up before dawn. The mist that had rolled in during the evening had thickened overnight, the heavy moisture had made sleeping almost impossible. He was feeling every bit his age and then some. Although his rise through the ranks had afforded him some creature comforts in the form of a private tent and a better cot than most of the others, he still was a restless sleeper and only rarely slept through the night.

He walked away from the campsite, down towards the creek. He had seen the sycamores when they arrived several days ago. They transported him away from this place, back in time – a simpler time. He felt like someone else, someone younger – more innocent - as he approached the water. It was brisk this morning. The leaves from the other trees had fallen, the sycamores stood out now. Winter wouldn't be far behind. He wondered how much snow this place saw. Probably not very much.

Dewey was up also; he had seen Henry leave his tent and walk down toward the stream. He followed, after giving Henry a little time to himself. As he finally approached Henry, Henry turned back smiling. Dewey could sense his moods. Dewey gave him space when he needed it, gave him his opinions when Henry asked – sometimes when he hadn't. He was still protecting Henry as he had been originally ordered to do, so long ago. Henry returned his gaze to the water, thinking, 'Would he ever have another friend like Dewey?'

He stood and turned back towards Dewey to say, 'Good morning'...

~

Jimmy Greaves could not stop shaking. The cool morning air was still foggy, and damp and he had shivered most of the night as he lay concealed out beyond his fellow rebel soldiers on the far-left flank of the army. As dawn approached, he was wide awake now. The lice were moving, and he began fidgeting. He was told to wait here last night until further orders came. He was also told not to shoot until ordered to.

He had only recently joined up and was assigned to Jubal Earlys' corps. Although only sixteen years old, he felt older. Some that he'd met were younger than him. He was the youngest of three brothers. His oldest brother, Caleb, had been killed at Sharpsburg defending a bridge in a cow pasture. His other brother, Michael, had been killed at Gettysburg. That left him to carry on. He wanted revenge. He wanted to kill every Yankee.

Caleb had shown him how to shoot. He'd also shown Michael, but Jimmy was better. Jimmy seemed to have more patience and paid closer attention to Caleb than Michael.

Jimmy heard some movement behind him. He had been told they'd be moving forward at daybreak. Down in the hollow he was in it was just beginning to become a little lighter. He could see a little further north towards the enemies' encampment just across the small creek that was out in front of him. He saw some movement; someone had come down to the water.

It was hard to make him out clearly. He raised his rifle and was looking at him with both eyes. In a moment he'd close one eye and take a shot – but not until the order to move across the creek had been given.

His Sergeant came up quietly behind him. "We're just about set boy."

Jimmy hoarsely whispered, "I got an officer down there near the water, upstream a piece."

The Sergeant thought for a moment. "You hold off for a minute or two. I'm going back to the boys. When we hear your shot, we'll all move forward. Understood?"

"Yes Sergeant." Jimmy replied. "Maybe he'll stand up and give me a better shot at him."

The Sergeant said. "No matter – you shoot a'fore five minutes goes by."

"Yes sir." Jimmy replied.

The Sergeant carefully moved back towards the rest of his men to explain the signal.

Jimmy continued to squint down along his rifle barrel at the blue belly. Jimmy waited and waited. It seemed like hours, but barely a minute had passed. He was just about to shoot anyway when the man began to stand up.

Jimmy eased off the trigger slightly. The officer looked to be straightening up. If he just turned slightly toward the creek, he would present a full profile target. Jimmies heart was racing, he decided to shoot. As his finger began to tighten on the trigger his target began to turn away from him. Jimmy yanked back against the trigger – not the best technique – not what Caleb had taught him.

~ 40 ~

Peter Fisher and the Judge had rapidly become close friends during his stay in July. When he left, he made arrangements to return in the fall. He'd been convinced that was the time to really enjoy the Glen, when the leaves began falling and the Sycamores stood out. He had spent nearly a week in Jasper and had thoroughly enjoyed his time with his new 'found' relatives. Although not a golfer, he enjoyed the pub at Sycamore Glen and everyone there quickly came to think of him as 'family' also.

Today he had driven the Judge up to the course and they were enjoying a late lunch. Ian was sitting with them in the corner booth, the Judges favorite table. As Peter looked out across the pond he said to Ian, "You know Ian, I envy you. Every day you come to work and get to look out there – at all that beauty."

Ian nodded, he looked at the Judge who was also nodding. He said to Peter, "When I first came here the course was just getting started. Even then you could tell this was going to be something special. The owners put everything they had into shaping this place – it shows. It's too bad they can't see it now."

The Judge chimed in, "When Charles and I bought it, we paid them their asking price. I think everyone came out ahead. They didn't lose money, and we've been able to make a go of it since then."

Peter said, "It looks like Mr. Steele has been able to keep things running pretty smoothly here."

"Well," the Judge said, "It was time for somebody younger to take over. Someone with a vision of the future. I agree, Dan has really done something special here."

Ian said, "Well he certainly has a way with people. I've been tending bar for some time now, and I don't think I've ever met anyone quite like him."

The Judge nodded in agreement. "I've met some pretty smooth operators in the legal system, but he'd put most of them to shame."

~ 41 ~

Dan had taken Claire out for dinner. While several other fine restaurants had opened in Jasper, as the building boom continued, they preferred Johnnies. Probably as much for sentimental reasons, as well as the food that Claire loved and that Dan, also seemed to prefer now. It also gave both of them an opportunity to catch up with their friends, Nancy and Russell.

This dinner invitation had caught Claire somewhat off guard, but that was Dan's style. As they enjoyed their meal, Claire tried to determine Dan's motives – without being overly obvious about it. Of course, Dan saw through this immediately, but played along, providing vague and contradictory answers to Claire's subtle interrogation of the reason behind the dinner date. They both enjoyed the sparring although neither would probably ever admit it.

Claire asked, "So - close any business deals recently?"

Dan chewed on his steak for a moment or two, "Yes, …No. Well …maybe …too soon to tell."

Claire thought to herself, 'Yup, he's got something up his sleeve.' – She pretended not to care, "Well I hope it works out."

Dan had thought there'd be more to this line of questioning. 'Huh' he thought – okay, I'll play along. "It'll probably come to nothing. How'd your day go? Any big news, any juicy municipal scandals I shouldn't know about?"

"About the same." she answered, pausing for effect, taking a long, slow, sip of her mixed drink – swirling the swizzle stick around the liquid and ice cubes. This forced Dan to stop chewing for several moments. "I may have something in the works. Probably too soon to get excited about it. I'll let you know how it goes."

"Well," he said, "I hope your deal works out too. Sometimes these things just take a bit of patience."

Claire nodded in agreement. She picked up the dessert menu and began nonchalantly looking down at the selections as Dan continued grinding on the last bite of his steak. She knew he'd ask about sharing a canola, figuring he'd get away with a half of the dessert and not risk the lecture on his weight by suggesting separates desserts. She tried a different tactic.

"I was thinking about having a piece of apple pie when you order the canola, that I know you love."

'Whoa!, where was this going?', he thought. She expects me to order something else – not an entire canola. She's baiting me to order the canola in order to discuss my diet – and feeble attempts at losing a little weight. But she must know I won't fall for this …his mind wandered off – trying to determine all the permutations of his possible answers.

As Nancy approached the table, Claire laid the menu back on the table. Nancy said hi to Dan, breaking into his computations.

All he said was, "Huh, oh hi Nancy. Gorgeous evening out there tonight, hope you're not working late."

Nancy smiled, "Thank you Dan. It is nice out there. Are you two having a good time?"

Claire responded, "We're having a great time. We're just deciding on dessert."

Nancy pulled her order pad from her apron and looked at Claire.

Claire said, "I'd like a slice of your apple pie, and Dan said he'd like a canola."

Nancy gave Dan a quizzical look as she wrote the order down. She was another of Claire's spies – like Mary – enlisted to help her watch his diet. "Just give me a couple minutes to warm the pie and I'll be back with them, okay?"

Dan nodded in agreement, puzzled about where this was headed. As Nancy walked away, Dan leaned across the table somewhat, to say to Claire a little quieter – "What's happening here?", challenging her - knowing his diet was at the root of all this.

Claire leaned across the table in response and said quietly, "I think we both know where this is headed." As she said this, she had reached her hand beneath the table and slid it up along his leg. High up along his leg …very high up.

Dan was mildly jolted by her touch – but stayed calm. Okay, now we've got a ballgame here. He stayed motionless for a moment or two, then leaned back in his seat, still not saying anything, squinting his eyes slightly at her. Preparing for the next volley.

Claire stayed leaning forward, inviting Dan to look down her blouse. After several moments, she too straightened up, pulling her shoulders back a bit, thrusting her chest forward …just enough.

She picked up her drink and sucked on the swizzle stick. There wasn't much fluid left in the glass. She kept sucking.

Dan stared at her then the glass. Finally, he said, "It's over.", and took the glass from her and sat it down on the table. When he looked back up into her face, she was pursing her lips.

"Maybe." Was all she said. The tip of her tongue came out slightly to run around the edge of her lips.

Dan had no response

Finally, she said, "I hope our desserts come soon, I think we have some more business to handle, at home, upstairs, where it's quiet, where we won't be disturbed …in the bedroom. We'll work on getting rid of the calories from the apple pie …and canola..

~ 42 ~

When Dan and Claire had returned from Johnnies, there was a large bouquet of flowers on the table in the foyer. Dan had also arranged for a vase of roses to be placed on Claire's nightstand. Mary had been only too happy to help out with the surprise.

When she entered the bedroom to change and saw the roses, her heart jumped a little. He really was something. At a party he could control a whole room full of people, and make you feel like you were the only one there – at the same time.

Dan had closed up the house, turning off the lights and locking the doors. When he came through the door into the bedroom several minutes later, Claire was waiting for him, wearing a sheer black nightgown that took his breath away.

She was not a teenager but had kept herself in great shape over the years. While no-one ever asked her about her age, all would have argued she was much younger than she would have to admit if under oath in a courtroom.

Although Dan was always being chided about losing a couple pounds, he just couldn't seem to do it. He wasn't obese, but he liked to say he was somewhere near the 'pudgy' marking on the 'porkiness' scale. Claire could not have cared less. Her concern was his over-all heath. Maybe this was his 'natural' weight.

She didn't mind a little 'thickness' to the sides of his torso. When he'd disrobed and climbed into bed beside her she was every bit as interested in how he looked as when he stared at her, as her nightgown had dropped to the floor ...

~

Later, as Claire and Dan lay in bed, exhausted from their efforts to lose a few calories, Claire had to smile.

When she'd first met Dan, she thought he was the biggest flirt she'd ever met. She wasn't wrong. He was still flirting with her. Even though they'd been married for five years, he was still flirting with her. He probably always would. And she loved it. 'It probably serves me right.', she thought. After the years of flirting following the death of her husband, Charles – she was getting a taste of her own medicine. She had not wanted to get too close to any man, but Dan was different. When he had come along, she was at a point in her life where she was vulnerable, wanting to share her life with someone again. Wanting to share the little joys and disasters of her daily routine, someone to be close to again. She had experienced the exuberant and erotic love of youth, and then the deep love of a committed marriage – and then it had all disappeared. She thought that she had seen the love of her life – that it had come ...and gone.

She was just beginning to realize that there was more to life, maybe not including romance, when Dan had come along. He was, in many ways, much like her. Although he had never married, he had told her that he felt that maybe he was beyond the stage in his life where he could ever feel really close to someone else.

But he was wrong, just like Claire. It probably helped that neither one had forced it to happen. Neither was trying to be someone, or something that they were not. It helped that they were nearly the same age. They were also both very astute business operators. They were successful in their fields and both were adept with the 'handling' of people.

~

She watched his breathing return to a steady rhythm as he began to relax. He was smiling as he rolled onto his side to face her.

"What are you grinning about?", she said with a smirky smile on her face.

"Oh, just thinking about how lucky I am.", he replied. He paused before continuing, "I just never pictured myself in a relationship like this."

"Why not?", she softly asked.

Carefully he answered, "I guess I never really tried to put the effort into it. I mean, I've had a lot of 'friends', some really close. But this is different – I suppose everybody feels this way at some point in their life when they've truly fallen in love with *the* right person."

Claire didn't speak, she could sense he had more to say.

"For a lot of years, I avoided getting too close to anybody. I know I haven't talked much about the war – I try not to – most people don't want to hear about any of it. But it changes you. It transforms you into something, or someone, you wouldn't ever want to become."

Claire was staring into his eyes now.

"Anyway, I'm surprised that all this has happened to me. I can't imagine ever being without you. I like who I've become. You've changed me."

Claire had tears rolling down her cheeks as she thought, 'He saved me, but here he is thanking me ….'. She drew herself in closer to him to lay her head on his chest and closed her eyes.

~

As Claire dreamed of the diary, Katie's voice interrupted her – 'My baby sister is going to have blue eyes! Blue eyes … Blue eyes…'

~

Dan gently shook her shoulder to wake her. She was startled out of her dream. Sunlight was pouring through the bedroom windows. Dan got up and made his way across the room, first to retrieve a bath robe and then into the bathroom to get a drink of water.

"You were having a nightmare. Sorry but I thought I should wake you." He said. "You were yelling out."

"Sorry." she said. "What was I saying?"

"Hard to tell. Something about blue eyes." He said.

Claire laughed and thought for a moment, "Well I was dreaming about the diary and out of nowhere I could hear Katie talking about having a sister with blue eyes! Isn't it weird what your mind goes through in a dream.?"

Dan said, "Oh yeah, I remember. That was the day Mary told everyone she was pregnant. Katie insisted she was going to have a sister with blue eyes – even though I explained that couldn't happen because Mary has brown eyes and Cletus has blue eyes."

Claire laughed again. "I'm sure Katie didn't understand …"

Dan started to say, "Well she's not old enough to …"

"What did you just say?" Claire blurted out as she sat up abruptly.

Dan looked at her for a moment, "Katie's only five, she wouldn't understand …"

"No before that!" insisted Claire who had stood up.

Dan replied, "I explained it was practically impossible for her to have blue eyes unless both Mary and Cletus had blue eyes. Because Mary had brown eyes – it is for all purposes impossible for a child of theirs to have blue eyes."

"Wait, wait, wait …" said Claire, "Does that mean that if both Mary and Cletus had blue eyes – their children would also have blue eyes?"

"Absolutely," said Dan, "It would be basically impossible that the children would have anything but blue eyes."

Claire left the room and came back with the diary that was in her office. Claire laid the diary down on the bed and opened it to a bookmarked page. Stuffed in the diary was a tinted picture of a man and a woman – both had blue eyes. Claire said "Look at this. It's a picture of Ruth and her husband Jedidiah – they both have blue eyes."

Dan took the picture and stared at it. "But this is hand colored. How can you be sure their eyes really are blue?"

"Turn it over." Claire said.

When Dan looked at the back side, there were the names, the hair colors -both brown, and the eye colors – both blue. "What does this mean Claire?"

"I've got a baby picture of my father sitting on his mother's lap – Clarissa. She had brown eyes."

"So, this means ..." started Dan.

"It means she can't be a child of Ruth and Jedidiah" said Claire.

"Wouldn't it mean that Ruth and ..." began Dan.

"Someone else fathered Clarissa." Finished Claire. "I mean if what you're saying about the odds ... is it really possible?"

Dan asked, "What color were Henry's eyes?"

July 1, 1888

Dewey stepped down off the train onto the station platform in Jasper. He turned to help his wife Carlotta, and then their daughter Sally, make the large step off the train down onto the platform. He looked around to find a porter to take their luggage into the station. Carlotta said to him, "Maybe we should just continue on. You don't even know if he's still alive."

Dewey looked at her and said, "Honey, relax. We've got plenty of time. There's no rush. Isn't this supposed to be a vacation for us?"

Carlotta smiled back. Dewey was right. They had plenty of time. Sally was moving to Philadelphia before starting school at Bryn Mawr in the fall. They were planning on staying with relatives of Dewey's until the middle of August. Dewey had to report to Washington regarding his next assignment and they had decided to combine everything else with a vacation as well.

A baggage handler was stacking their bags on the platform as Dewey walked into the station. Sally said to her mother, "Mom, do you think this is going to work out? I don't mind going to school closer to home. They say that Stanford University will be opening soon. I could wait ..."

"Absolutely not!" was Carlotta's answer. "I won't have you going to school with boys. Besides, I don't want you waiting to start school, you should go now while you're young before you meet someone, get married and forget all about school. No. This will work out."

Dewey came back out and said to them, "They're bringing our bags around to a carriage that'll take us to the hotel."

Carlotta gathered up her shirts as did Sally, and they made their way across the platform into the station.

Dewey went back to the stationmaster. "Excuse me sir …" The stationmaster looked up. "You wouldn't happen to know of a Henry Hawkins that might be living nearby, would you?"

The stationmaster shook his head, "No sir, sorry. The last name sounds familiar, but I've only been here a short time. You should ask at the hotel or across the square at Bartlett's Dry Goods store. Mr. Bartlett knows everyone here 'bouts. He'll be able to tell you if the person you're looking for lives in Jasper."

Henry thanked him and joined Carlotta and Sally as they walked out the door towards the carriage. Henry asked the driver to take them to the hotel. Jasper didn't look big enough to have more than one hotel. Dewey had been surprised when he found out that the rail line came through Jasper. When he'd known Henry, Henry had said Jasper was a small village and didn't have rail service. But that was years ago … a lifetime.

The driver helped with the baggage at the hotel. He had noticed a slight limp when the middle-aged man walked arm in arm with his wife as they moved from the carriage towards the hotel. Once inside, Dewey arranged for a small suite of three rooms on the top floor of the three-story hotel. The sitting room looked out over the town square. There was a small bandstand and children were playing in the large grassy expanse.

Dewey suggested that Carlotta and Sally rest for a while before they had dinner. The trip from California had been taxing on Carlotta and Sally, but to Dewey, it was a luxurious ride. He had originally crossed the country on horseback. Moving from fort to fort with his troops. He had only rarely taken a train. He said to Carlotta, "I'm going to ask around a bit about Henry. I won't be long. Try and get a little rest, okay?"

Carlotta smiled, "We'll be okay, go stretch your legs. I know you hate sitting for any length of time. Just don't forget us here okay?" she finished with a twinkle in her eye. "Don't do too much exploring."

Dewey laughed. She knew him well. "I won't be long. I'll find a place for dinner as well."

He left the hotel and Carlotta watched as he crossed the square heading for the business' she could see, opposite the hotel. Sally was watching too, "Is dad okay? He seems kind of quiet."

Carlotta was still watching Dewey, she said to Sally, "This is important to him dear. I hope he finds Mr. Hawkins. I hate to think what this will do to him if he doesn't."

~

Dewey was in his stride now. His leg was loosening up, he had sat too long on the train. He should have moved about more, rather than sitting and staring out the windows.

Ralph Bartlett watched from his storefront as Dewey made his way across the square towards the store. Dewey climbed the steps and said hi to Ralph, "Afternoon sir."

Ralph returned the greeting, "Same to you sir, how can I help you?" Ralph edged back into the store with Dewey close behind. The inside of the store was a little darker and there was a stove back in the corner with a small group of people gathered around in quiet conversation. Even though it was July these folks just couldn't break the habit of sitting around the stove – even when it wasn't lit. One was asleep with a hat slouched down over his face.

Dewey said to Ralph, "Well sir, maybe you can help me locate someone that used to live here. The stationmaster said you're the one I should talk to."

Ralph chuckled, "Suppose so, been 'round here long enough to know most everyone. Who is it you're trying to find?"

Dewey said, "Henry Hawkins sir. I served under him in the war, I just thought I'd see how he was doing, if he lived here. It's been more than twenty-five years. I didn't know much about him, but he said he was from Jasper. I'm on my way east ...."

"Hawkins, you say?" replied Ralph. "Hawkins? Now that you mention it, yes, seems as though I did know him. He was coming through here before the war looking for work. I recollect that I sent him up to Sycamore Hill to talk to a farmer up there." Ralph came out from behind the counter and motioned for Dewey to follow him over to the stove. As they approached, the men in conversation looked up. "Any of you know of a Henry Hawkins?" said Ralph. The men looked at each other with a variety of non-committal movements of their heads. Ralph leaned down to the person who appeared to have nodded off to sleep. "What about you?" he said while lightly tapping the man's shoulder.

The man was somewhat startled and began slowly raising his head as you would when awakening, careful not to hurt your neck any more than it already felt.

Dewey said to him, "I'm trying to find an old friend of mine named Henry Hawkins. Is there any chance you know of him or where I might find him?"

As the man looked up from beneath the wide brim of his hat he said, "Well son, it does appear that your eyesight has finally failed you. Not that it was ever that good!"

Dewey's eyes teared up uncontrollably as Henry spoke. Henry moved his hat back and stood slowly to shake Dewey's hand. Dewey took it and pumped it vigorously. The men began laughing as Dewey let go of Henry's hand and hugged him.

Henry took a step back and looked at Dewey. "Boys let me introduce to you Dewey Carson, an old friend of mine. You look good Dewey – or should I say General Carson?"

"Dewey's fine with me Henry. Maybe I should be addressing you as Colonel Hawkins?"

With that there was more laughing as Dewey sat down beside Henry.

"Dewey, what brings you to our neck of the woods? You lost again?"

Dewey said, "No, I came by train. Hard to get lost riding one of them."

Henry said, "I thought I'd never see you again. This is really something. How long are you staying? You're not leaving right away, are you?"

Dewey said, "Carlotta and I are taking our daughter, Sally, east to stay with my relatives. She's starting school this fall in Philadelphia."

Henry was processing this as he stood, "Your daughter Sally .... Carlotta? They're here? Where? ...

Dewey said, "We're at the hotel. We just came in on the train ..."

Henry said, "Well I hope you haven't unpacked. You've got to come up to the mill and stay with us. Ruth has to meet you, Clarissa too. After all I've told them about you ..." Henry grabbed Dewey's arm leading him out of the store. "Come on, my wagon is just outside here, I was just getting set to go back up the hill – must have dozed off for a bit." There was some laughter behind them as they went through the doorway out into the street.

They continued out across the square towards the hotel. When they entered, the desk clerk caught the attention of Dewey, "Sir, you have a telegram." He retrieved it from the mail rack behind the counter and handed it to Dewey. "The stationmaster hopes you don't mind, but when it came in, he answered the sender that you and your family had arrived safely. If you like, I can have a boy take a message back and have it sent. Afternoon Colonel." He added as he saw who was accompanying his guest.

Dewey opened the envelope and smiled. He said to Henry, "It's just Captain Fisher. Checking to make sure we made it this far. He's my adjutant. Fine man." He thanked the clerk as he and Henry stepped back from the desk towards the stairs.

Henry was processing the name ...

Dewey said, "Yup. Best left-handed shot in the army. Trained him myself ...well, sort of. Had a little help early on."

Henry chuckled, "So, you were listening to all that I told you? Able to pass a little of it on, I suppose!"

Dewey said, "Every word. Probably saved my life on more than one or two occasions."

~ 43 ~

The late November day was warmer than usual. There had been a couple of bursts of cooler weather already, but the prediction was for a stretch of clear weather with very little chance of any rain. As Ian looked out over the golf course from MacGregor's, he could see the bold colors of the hardwoods on the hill dominating the still vibrant green expanse of the holes woven around the trees on the hillside. The business had been brisk today, even though it was the middle of the week.

Cletus had arranged with Ian to look after Katie today when she was finished with school. Mary's pregnancy was nearing term, and Cletus was trying to get Mary to take some more time off during the final weeks before the birth of their child. Ian would never say no to watching Katie. They were 'best friends', Katie shared everything with 'Poppy'. When Cletus and Katie came into MacGregor's she was on a dead run to tell Poppy all about her day at school. Ian laughingly waved Cletus off, sure that he had things to do out on the course before the end of the day.

All Cletus could say was a quick 'Thanks' as Katie began pouring out the day's events for Ian. She climbed up into her chair by the window, while Ian got her a glass of milk from the kitchen to go along with a big chocolate chip cookie from the batch that Terry had baked earlier in the day.

As she was eating her cookie, Ian asked her if she wanted to ride up the hill with him to visit the waterfall. Of course, she'd said 'Yes' as she gulped down the last of her milk. Ian stepped into the kitchen to let Terry know he'd be back in a little bit. Bruce would be in shortly – there was only an elderly couple in the restaurant finishing a late lunch. Susan would also be in soon, so everything would continue to run smoothly in MacGregor's.

Ian and Katie walked out past Curtis, and Ian mentioned he was taking a cart for the trip up the hill. They'd be back shortly. They walked to the carts grouped outside the door, chose one, and made their way around the pond towards the edge of the course. Crossing over Sycamore Creek, they followed the trail heading up through the Glen.

Ian and Katie had made it up the hill to the maintenance shed when Ian suggested they walk the rest of the way to the waterfall. The woods were so quiet as they approached the waterfall. The sounds of the golf carts on the course had faded away, all you could hear was the slight rustling of the leaves as a breeze swirled across the hillside. Squirrels and blue jays made it known that there were intruders in their domain, but their protests were half-hearted. While Ian didn't visit often, Katie was practically a fixture in the woods between her house at the top of the hill and the golf course.

As they approached the waterfall, Ian had to catch his breath. It was so beautiful here. He had to remind himself to come up here more often. Some of the leaves were beginning to fall and they covered the small pond beneath the waterfall. The mosaic of yellow, red, and orange splotches of color on the water was stunning.

As Ian leaned back to look high up into the sycamores at the light filtering down to the water, he felt a little light-headed. He became dizzier as rays of the warm sunlight fell on his face. The cool breeze, the mixture of soft scents of the woods, it all felt so …
Blackness

Ian laid there and opened his eyes, looking up into the sycamores ...through them ...the dazzling light ...thoughts of Katherine flooded his mind ...she was with him again ... Blackness

Looking downward from above the tops of the sycamores at the upper pond, Ian could see a young woman sitting on the millstone under the sycamore next to the pond. She had a book. She wasn't reading. She was writing ... Blackness ...

~ 44 ~

Curtis was at his desk when the phone rang. He knew from the double ring that it was the phone at the maintenance shed. When he answered, Katie was on the other end. The words were pouring out of her faster than he could comprehend.

"Katie, this is Curtis. Slow down a little, what's happening?"

"Poppy fell down on the ground. He won't get up!"

Curtis said, "Is he hurt? Is he bleeding? Can he talk?"

"Poppy is talking, but I don't know what he's saying."

Curtis continued, "Where is he? Is he with you by the telephone?"

"No, he's by the waterfall."

"Katie, we'll be there in a couple minutes. You can stay with me on the phone, until your daddy gets there. Okay?"

"I'm going back to be with Poppy." The line went dead.

Curtis called the Jasper Fire Department to get an ambulance up to Cletus' and Mary's house above the waterfall. That would be the closest way they could get a vehicle to Ian. He called Cletus' office but there was no answer. He turned to look out the window to see if he was anywhere in sight. He couldn't see him anywhere. He went into Dan's office and found Teddy there with Dan.

Curtis blurted out, "Something's happened to Ian up at the waterfall. Katie just called. I think it sounds like a stroke. I've got an ambulance headed up to the house. I can't find Cletus, he's out on the course some place."

Without hesitation Teddy said, "Sound the lightening alarm horn, just three quick blasts – not the longer pattern we use for a storm. That'll bring him here quick."

Dan was next, "I'm heading up there with my truck. Tell Cletus we'll meet him up there. We may be able to get Ian to the house faster than they can make their way down to the waterfall. Call Mary and tell her what's happening, she can tell the firemen how to get down to the waterfall if we haven't already brought Ian to them."

As Dan and Teddy raced out to Dan's truck, Curtis sounded the alarm. Golfers throughout the course stopped what they were doing, wondering why the alarm would sound, there wasn't a cloud in the sky.

~ 45 ~

Cletus was on the course on hole number 4 removing a limb that had fallen across a cart path overnight. When he heard the sharp, blasts of the horn that was normally used to alert the golfers to the threat of lightening, he knew it was serious. Teddy had worked this out as a signal, so that anyone working out on the course should return to the clubhouse. He dropped the debris he was loading into his cart, and immediately headed toward the clubhouse.

Coming down the fairway he caught a glimpse of Dan's red pickup headed up the hill along the path by the creek. He veered across the course to try to catch up with Dan. He went straight up the number 14 fairway to cross the creek using the bridge near the green. When he got there, he could see that Dan had continued up the path towards the waterfall. His truck had knocked down the underbrush along either side of the narrow path that Cletus had hacked out leading up the hill to their house.

All Cletus could think of was the pond. Katie must have fallen into it.

When he arrived at the waterfall, Dan and Teddy were carrying Ian to the truck. Cletus helped them lift Ian into the bed of the truck and jumped in beside Teddy – Dan got Katie into the cab of the truck while Teddy and Cletus were trying to get Ian comfortable. Immediately, Dan continued up the hill.

He drove carefully not wanting to injure Ian any more than he already was. Cletus had yelled forward to Dan that Ian was conscious and able to talk somewhat.

It only took them a couple of minutes to reach the upper pond. As they crossed the field towards the house, Cletus could see an ambulance arriving, pulling around the house towards the pond.

As the ambulance crew got out of their vehicle, Mary joined them to explain that something had happened to her father, Ian.

In Jasper, everyone knew everybody else. Mary knew both firemen, and that Ian was in good hands as they moved him from the truck onto a stretcher, then into the ambulance, for the trip to the hospital. While Ian was conscious, he was having trouble speaking and this was frustrating him. Mary climbed into the ambulance with Ian after telling Katie to stay with her Daddy.

.

July 1, 1888

afternoon

Dewey and Henry walked up the three flights of stairs to Dewey's rooms. Henry noticed Dewey limping as they climbed the final section of stairs. Henry said to Dewey, "That injury from Culps Hill acting up?"

Dewey stopped and turned as he finished with the stairs, "What injury? I just twisted my foot in that muck."

"Dewey, I didn't believe it then, and I still don't believe it now. I'm glad the bullet just grazed you. Putting a little mud on it was probably a good thing to do, though it didn't hide the hole in your boot very well." Said Henry with a chuckle as he continued past Dewey.

Dewey followed, then passed Henry to open his door into the suite. The room was empty when they entered. "Carlotta and Sally must be lying down." Said Dewey as he quietly opened first, one-bedroom door, then the other. Both rooms were empty.

Dewey looked across at Henry.

Henry said, "Looks as though you've lost your women." Henry had remained just inside the doorway near the windows that looked out onto the square. He looked out towards the bandstand that was on the farther end of the green expanse. "Any chance those two handsome women out there by the bandstand are related to you?"

Dewey came over to the window. "I see your eyesight hasn't changed." While Dewey continued looking out the window, the two women began moving back towards the hotel. He said to Henry, "They must have spotted us coming across to the hotel, they're coming back also."

Henry said, "See if they've unpacked. If they haven't, we can go right up to the mill."

Dewey looked into the bedrooms again, "Doesn't look as though they unpacked much of anything. I thought they would want to rest a bit before we found a place to have dinner."

Henry pulled a watch from his pocket, "It's just past two, we'll have plenty of time to make it back up to the mill. We have more than enough room for you up there. We can spend a little time together before you leave, assuming you have room in your schedule."

Dewey said, "Well, we have some time, there's no big rush. I didn't know how long it would take to find you, or if you had settled someplace else after the war. I assumed you'd made it through …well …that you'd survived."

Henry said, "Thanks to you. Yes. They sent me home for a while. I came back here. A lot had changed. Ruth looked after me. Then I was called back to Washington. They kept me behind a desk until the war ended. I left the army, I was never going to make a career of it. Apparently not like you."

Dewey smiled, "Yeah, I've stayed with it. I never would have met Carlotta if I hadn't been in the army and been sent out west. It's our life, as long as Carlotta doesn't mind the moving around …well, I'll be retiring before too much longer. It's a young man's profession. After we drop Sally off with my sister in Philadelphia, we'll be in Washington to find out what's next for us."

The two men were standing by the window finding all about what had happened in the last twenty-five years of each other's lives. Neither man noticed the two women standing just outside the doorway. They had quietly come up to the doorway and were mesmerized by the conversation taking place. After several moments,

Carlotta politely interrupted, "I do declare that I've never heard you speak that much about yourself Andrew Carson!"

Dewey was startled, "Carlotta, Sally – come in. I want you to meet the Colonel, Henry – Henry Hawkins!"

Henry had been wearing his slouch hat, but quickly removed it while he approached Carlotta and Sally as they entered the room.

"Henry – this is my wife Carlotta and our daughter Sally."

Henry said, "Ma'am, I've so very pleased to meet you and your daughter." He reached out to shake Carlotta's hand, but she moved closer and hugged Henry tightly.

As Carlotta moved away from Henry she said, "Mr. Hawkins, I can't begin to tell you how very much it means to me to finally meet you. To thank you for everything you've done for Andrew …we wouldn't be a family if not for you!"

Carlotta was tearing up, she hugged Henry again.

Sally moved closer to her mother. She said to Henry, "Mother's right Mr. Hawkins. I've grown up hearing dad talk about you. I'm honored to meet you. Thank you."

Henry was blushing, almost at a loss for words. "Ladies, it's you I that have to thank. Thank you for taking care of someone who I care so very much about, and I'm so glad you've accompanied him here to find me." Then he added with a big grin, "I also have to thank you for finally telling me what his name is. I knew it couldn't be Dewey, but I figured I'd let him tell me when he was good and ready."

Everyone laughed.

Sally said to Henry, "Dad's always told us that his baby sister Sally, my namesake, tried to say 'Andrew', but couldn't pronounce r's so she called him Andew, but after a while she just called him Dewey."

Henry was laughing now. He looked at Dewey, "Well your secret's safe with me. If it's all the same, I'm going to stick with Dewey."

Dewey just nodded that it was okay with him.

"But, while we're talking about names," as he looked at Carlotta then Sally, "please, call me Henry. I wouldn't know how to answer to 'Mr. Hawkins', everyone here 'bouts just calls me Henry."

Dewey looked at him, "I heard the clerk downstairs address you as 'Colonel'".

Henry frowned, "Yeah I get called that around here sometimes. I know they mean well, but I prefer Henry. I've given up asking them to just call me Henry."

Carlotta said, "Well I'm sure it's intended as a sign of respect. I think Andrew tires of it sometimes, but I can see respect in those that deal with Andrew, with or without the 'General' being used."

Henry said, "Well ma'am, your husband tells me that you and your daughter haven't unpacked much yet. I was hoping to have you come up to the mill and stay with us while you're here. Ruth and Clarissa will love having some guests. We've more than enough room. I can bring the wagon around, if you're up for a small trip this afternoon."

Carlotta looked to Dewey and nodded 'yes'. She said, "We'd love to Henry, as long as it won't be an imposition."

"Nonsense," said Henry. "It'll be a little cooler up on the hill. You'll love it up there, everyone does that's visited. Besides, Clarissa's not much older than Sally – I'm sure Sally doesn't want to spend all her time listening to more war stories – she'll have some fun up there before she's off to school."

With everyone in agreement, Henry set off to retrieve the wagon while the Carson family repacked for the trip up to Sycamore Glen.

~ 46 ~

At the hospital, Ian was rushed into an emergency room where doctors began monitoring his vital signs and tried to determine what had happened to him. It seemed apparent that he'd suffered a stroke. There was a new theory making the rounds in the medical journals that proposed treating a stroke patient with a large dose of aspirin as soon as possible in the case of a stroke.

Ian was alert and cognizant of everything going on around him. He was just frustrated that he couldn't clearly communicate with everyone trying to treat him. Mary was by his side; he was concerned about the added stress on Mary – her due date was fast approaching.

Cletus took Katie back to their house and tried to explain to her that Poppy was sick and had to go the hospital so the doctors there could make him feel better. Katie understood about hospitals, Cletus and Mary had started explaining to her that her Mommy would have to go to the hospital when the baby was born. The doctors there would help Mommy feel better. They hadn't gone much further than that, they just wanted her to know that the hospital wasn't a bad place. That people went there all the time so that the doctors could help them feel better.

Curtis called to say that he had talked to Susan about coming up to take care of Katie so that Cletus could go to the hospital. He'd also spoken with Terry and Bruce who would take care of MacGregor's until more was known about Ian's condition.

After Cletus had hung up, it wasn't long before Dan knocked on the door. He'd come up to not just check on Katie, but also to see how Cletus was taking all this. He knew that Cletus had grown distant from his parents. Although both were still alive, they hadn't made the effort to visit Cletus, even after he had written them to tell them about their grandchild. All this had caused Cletus to become much closer to Ian than what might otherwise be the case between a son-in-law and a father-in-law.

Dan told Cletus he'd stay with Katie until Susan arrived, which probably wasn't going to be much longer. Cletus changed out of his work clothes, cleaned up a little, and left for the hospital.

~ 48 ~

When Cletus arrived at the hospital, he found Mary in the waiting area adjacent to the Emergency Room entrance. She looked like she was holding up okay – she came over to Cletus as he came through the doorway.

"The doctors say he is doing okay. They don't think it was anything to do with his heart. Most likely a mild stroke. They want to keep him connected to the monitors for several hours before moving him to a room."

Cletus was visibly relieved, "How are you doing?"

"Cletus, I'm okay. What'd you tell Katie about Poppy?"

"I told her that he was sick and needed to go to the hospital where doctors could make him feel better."

Mary said, "Katie probably saved his life by calling. I'm glad he took her with him up there."

Cletus said to her, "Come on, sit down over here."

The two crossed the room to chairs set against the far wall. Cletus watched as Mary gingerly sat down.

"Mary how are you, really?" Said Cletus with an imploring look. Mary looked edgy, not quite herself.

"Cletus, I'm doing fine. I can't stand too long, but other than that, I'm okay, really." She said with a forced look of bravado.

Cletus said to her, "I could see if Doctor Casey is here. He could take a quick look at you. Do you want me to call him?"

Mary hesitated for a moment before telling Cletus 'No.', that she didn't think it was necessary. That little hesitation was all it took for Cletus. He went to the desk to see if they could page Doctor Casey – to see if he was already in the hospital. When he phoned back a couple minutes later, Cletus explained the situation and the doctor said he'd stop in to see Mary when he was through with the patient he was currently with. Cletus returned to Mary's side.

As Mary's pregnancy had progressed, Doctor Casey was having a hard time with the baby's heartbeat. It appeared to be fairly strong but at times there appeared to be an 'echo', he was monitoring her progress closely. He had seen this condition several times in his young career. It wasn't serious, but he felt it would be best to keep his thoughts to himself a little while longer.

July 1, 1888

evening

When Henry returned to the mill that afternoon, Ruth was thrilled to meet Dewey and his family. The mill had been a large operation and the building had expanded over the years to also include additional rooms that Isaac had let out for additional income. Currently there were no boarders, Henry and Ruth had shied away from keeping the rooms filled.

Their lives were quiet ones. The mill work was in decline. They were still showing a profit from it, but most of the farmers now had their milling done in nearby Bingley. Henry and Ruth were always busy, they had found ways of supplementing their income. Henry by using the tools in the machine shop to make and fix a wide variety of farm implements while Ruth did extensive baking, since the meager profits from the milling business were usually in the form of a percentage of the milled product.

When introducing Ruth and Clarissa to Dewey, Carlotta and Sally, Henry included Tavis McDonald in the introductions. Tavis was the only full-time employee at the mill and lived there as well. It never took very long for anyone to realize that Tavis was more than just a hired employee. He and Henry were together constantly. Because of Henry's war injury, he relied on Tavis for lifting anything heavy around the mill – which was quite often the case. Although Henry did not have a son, you would not have guessed that if you spent any time around the two of them.

~

When Tavis had first come across from Scotland he had followed the rail line west looking for work. When he came through Jasper, and made it known that he had experience working in a mill, Josiah jumped at the chance to hire him. Isaac and Josiah had not been a close father and son team at the mill. Since marrying Sarah, Josiah wanted nothing more than to live the life of a farmer with Sarah – away from the mill. Isaac had died near the end of the war leaving everything to Josiah. While he ran the mill, he preferred farming. When Henry returned to Jasper after the war he went to work for Josiah at the mill.

As Henry and Ruth slowly fell in love, Josiah convinced Henry to take over the mill. As a wedding present, Henry and Ruth received the mill and the immediate property surrounding it.

~

That night Henry invited Sarah, Josiah, and their daughter Mary, down to the mill to join them for supper and meet Dewey, Carlotta and Sally. While they were all around the table eating, Henry looked around the table thinking, 'This is how it should be. All the people I care most about, enjoying each other's company and the meal that Ruth and Clarissa had prepared. Life really couldn't get much better than this.

July 2, 1888

morning

The next morning Henry took Dewey for a walk up through the glen to the waterfall and beyond, to the upper pond. It was a walk Henry had made countless times, but always enjoyed. Walking through the lower meadow near the creek, the meadowlarks were singing, practically welcoming you to their domain. Further up the hill nearer the hardwoods it became quieter with only the sound of the trickling water in the nearly dry creek bed to mark their cadence as they walked.

Dewey was the first to break the silence, "Henry you truly live in paradise here. I'd listen to you talk about all this only on rare occasions – you'd always say, 'Don't think about what you left behind, stay focused on what you're doing here.' I see now how difficult it must have been for you to tell me that, having all this waiting for you."

Henry nodded, "I tried to keep it buried while we were out there. But you're right, it was hard. I'm sure you saw thru me on more than a couple occasions."

Dewey said, "Definitely at Cedar Creek, I can understand why, when I see these sycamores along the creek."

Henry looked at one as they passed into the woods. "Wait until you see the one at the top of the hill, it's gigantic."

The two walked along the creek quietly for several minutes.

Henry said, "Twenty-five years ago today …Culps Hill …"

Dewey responded, "Yeah, that's what I was thinking when I got up this morning …"

The two walked up to the waterfall and stopped, staring into the pond. Only a small amount of water was falling over the ledge into the pool beneath it. The pond skippers were out in force, you could easily trace their paths across the pond. The air stagnant, the musty odor of the exposed rocks that had been underwater until recently, caught in your throat …reminding you ...

After several quiet moments Henry turned to face Dewey, "Can you ever forgive me for ordering you down into that mire below Culps Hill with your men?"

Dewey's head snapped up from looking into the pool. He too had let his mind wander back … He faced Henry, "It was your job, it was my job, it was our job. Every one of us knew then, and those of us that are still alive, know now. It was what was required of us."

Henry started to shake his head.

Dewey saw this, "Henry, put it behind you. I've had to – many times over the years. Don't let it eat you up. Without men like you, we would have lost the damn war. Pure and simple."

Henry tried to look at Dewey … was hesitant.

Dewey said, "You have a lovely wife, a beautiful daughter …everyone here respects you. You're at the very heart of this community."

Henry was thinking through this as he looked at Dewey.

Dewey said, "Is there anything in particular bringing this on, other than, well …you know, twenty-five years ago?"

Henry thought for a moment, "That's mostly the reason. I know there's talk of putting a statue up, the battles we fought in and all that. I don't like it!"

Dewey said, "I'm sure everyone here is just trying to find a way of thanking you, that's all."

Henry said, "I don't like it. I don't want a statue."

Dewey wasn't going to press Henry on this. So, he changed the subject. "I thought you were taking me up here to see a pond with some big sycamore nearby."

Henry chuckled and thought to himself, 'Still the same old Dewey – looking out for him'. He said to Dewey, "Well, we'll have to hike up the hill a bit further. Will your feeble legs hold out a little longer? Come on, follow me."

With that, the two continued their hike through the woods, just like hikes they'd taken together years before – it didn't seem that long ago though. To old soldiers, it never does.

July 2, 1888

mid-morning

Henry and Dewey arrived at the upper pond after another long conversation about what the two had done over the last twenty-five years. Dewey had been sent west, skipping across the plains from fort to fort. In late 1868 he'd arrived at the Presidio of San Francisco, and later fought in the Modoc Indian Campaign. While not talking much about his military actions there, he gushed when speaking about how he met Carlotta.

She was a true Californian; her parents were first generation Californians whose parents had come from Spain to settle in the Mexican territory of California. Her grandparents later aligned themselves with the Americans to fight against the Mexicans for their freedom from the harsh Mexican rule.

Dewey was stunned by her beauty when he was introduced to her at a formal dinner held when the newly arrived military commander, Major General Thomas, was introduced to the Californian social set. Her father was Rafael Sebastian, a true Californian patriot who had fought with Fremont against the Mexicans.

Although still quite young, Carlotta was an accomplished rider and was often seen riding far from her home overlooking the Pacific Ocean south of the Presidio. Dewey had made it his business to become familiar with the countryside surrounding her home, particularly the riding trails. After several 'chance' encounters with

Carlotta, Dewey sensed that she liked him enough to perhaps have arranged one or two of the meetings on her own. Shortly afterward, Dewey visited privately with Rafael to secure permission to court Carlotta. Rafael was neither blind, nor a fool. While he doted on Carlotta, he had come to like Dewey during the many occasions that the military met with influential citizens, such as Rafael, in the course of the military transfer of responsibilities following the war, back to the elected civil authorities.

The marriage of Carlotta to Dewey in 1869 was the high point of the social season. While Rafael would miss Carlotta as she moved with Dewey as his assignments changed, he knew she was a free spirit – this is what she longed for.

Sally had come along that next year. But it had not slowed down the movement of the Carson family. Dewey's assignments had moved them all about the west coast.

Now, with Sally going to school in the east, Carlotta and Dewey had started to think about life after the army. They would probably settle in California; Carlotta had many relatives there. But then again you could never tell what might strike their fancy – it would probably depend on where Sally settled after school.

As Henry and Dewey approached the pond, Dewey involuntarily stared up at the massive sycamore. Then he looked out across the pond towards the farmhouse where Josiah and Sarah lived. When he turned to face Henry, Henry was smiling.

"It's really something up here. Isn't it?", he said to Dewey.

Dewey was nodding his head, taking in the full sweep of everything surrounding the pond. "Henry, I thought the lower part of the Glen was so nice. But up here …"

Henry said to Dewey, "This is where I came to work for Ezekiel when I first came to Jasper. I helped plow the fields out there." He said with a wave of his arm encompassing the large field beyond the pond that stretched to distant woods. "Later we'd bring the crops in, storing everything over there in the barn." Henry pointed back towards the farmhouse and the barn behind it..

As Dewey looked back in that direction, Sarah was coming out of the house. She saw them by the pond and waved before going around the corner of the farmhouse towards the barn.

Henry and Dewey waved back.

"Henry, whatever became of Jack?"

This brought a broad smile to Henry's face. "Hardly a day goes by that I don't think of Jack. After the war, I returned, and we had some good times. I gave up farming here for Ezekiel to work for Josiah down at the mill. I decided Jack deserved some quality time after the hard years working for Ezekiel – so Jack retired."

Henry pointed over towards the barn, "I kept him in the paddock over there most of the time. He was down at the mill during the busy season in the fall, closer to me. But I think he preferred it up here. Sarah said he'd stand over there in the corner of the paddock where he could look across here to the pond, while I was gone."

Dewey agreed, "Well I can't blame him for wanting to see this every day."

Henry laughed. "That's what I thought too. One day I came up here in the morning to see him and when I looked across there, he wasn't standing in the corner. When I got to the paddock he was down. I never knew how old he was, but ..."

Dewey stayed quiet.

"Anyway, he was my best friend for a lot of years. I talked to Josiah and he let me bury Jack here where he liked it best." Henry nodded back behind where they were standing, back towards the sycamore.

Dewey turned back toward the tree. "There?" he said.

Henry nodded. They took a couple steps back towards the mill stone beneath the tree. "I had a set of stones that I knew we'd never use at the mill. I asked around about someone buying them. No one was interested. They were just lying there. I brought this one up here, I figured it'd keep him protected."

Henry continued, "Isaac always had a lot of plans for the mill. He and Ezekiel were always scheming about something. Isaac wanted to expand the mill, use a bigger set of stones. But the way the wheel is set up – as an undershot – there just wouldn't have been enough power to turn stones this big in diameter. Maybe bigger than what we're using now, but not this big. Just another of Isaacs' crazy ideas that didn't pan out."

July 2, 1888

late morning

Later as Henry and Dewey were walking back down through the Glen to the mill, Tavis met up with them near the waterfall.

"Miss Ruth asked me to come find you two." He said with a smile. "Seems as though she thought you might be lost up here."

That brought a smile to Henry's face and he said, "Yeah, when I'm gone for more than an hour, she figures I'm lost someplace."

Dewey laughed, "I get that from Carlotta too. I think it's in a wife's nature – always knowing where her husband is."

Dewey gave Henry a sly look, then said to Tavis, "How about you son, is there anyone in particular around here that's caught your eye? Someone that might think you're lost?"

Tavis hesitated, then replied, "Well sir there is someone ...he hesitated ..."

"Dewey," said Henry, "the fact that Tavis here is sweet on Mary Mueller, has to be one of the worst kept secrets in the Glen, or Jasper too, for that matter."

Tavis's face started to turn red. He began, "Sir ...".

Henry cut him off. "Tavis, first off its Henry ..." He gave Dewey a look of exasperation before turning back to Tavis to continue, "Secondly, any damn fool who's not blind can see that you're in love with her. And I seem to notice an extra twinkle in her eyes when you're anywhere nearby."

Tavis looked at Dewey who smiled and nodded in agreement with Henry.

Tavis started over, "Sir ...Henry ...I hope you don't think that Mary ... I mean Miss Mueller, and I are ..."

Henry put his hand up to stop Tavis, "Whoa up there son. I'm sure you two are behaving." He chuckled, "Besides, I know Josiah and Sarah are keeping a pretty close eye on you two."

Dewey joined in, "I know we've just met, and I've only been here a short time, but Tavis, if you don't mind me saying, aside from how Mary acts around you – it's also pretty obvious that Sarah and Josiah are pretty fond of you also. I'd guess that at some point in the future they'd welcome you into the family as a son-in-law."

~ 49 ~

When Dr. Casey finally made it into the waiting room to see Mary, she was showing obvious signs of discomfort. She was fidgeting around, sitting, standing then sitting again. She was glad when he popped around the corner into the waiting area.

"So, how's my favorite patient doing today?" His voice boomed out. "I checked on Ian on my way through, he looked to be stable, he managed a smile when I said 'Hi' to him. Word travels fast when a new patient comes in."

Mary stood, "They asked me to wait here while they moved him to a room. Is he in a room now?"

Casey answered, "They were just finishing up moving him. I'm sure you'll be able to see him in a couple of minutes."

Cletus looked questionably at the doctor, Casey took the signal – "The real question Mrs. Armstrong, is, how are you doing?"

Mary gave him a weak smile, "I've okay. I'm just concerned about Dad."

Dr. Casey responded, "Well he's doing just fine. I don't want you to get yourself worked up – the doctors want to keep him under observation for a while – probably not more than a day or two. Dr. Spafford is the cardiologist on call tonight. I'm sure Ian's receiving the best care." While talking with Mary, he was going through a mental checklist of items that he performed each time he encountered one of his obstetrics patients. Based on his observations, it appeared that she needed a closer exam.

"Mary, why don't we get you into an examination room where I can check you over a little more closely – listen to the baby's heart? It'll only take a minute. It'll be a couple more minutes before you can get into to see Ian."

Mary glanced towards Cletus and nodded as she began to get back to her feet.

She said to Dr. Casey, "I think it's a good idea, I'm feeling …"

Mary took a small step backwards to catch her balance. Cletus was by her side and steadied her as she straightened up.

The doctor was also in motion, he turned back towards the reception desk and calmly, but firmly, asked the nurse for a wheelchair.

The nurse had taken in the situation and was already bringing a wheelchair from around her counter and met Mary before she had taken many steps.

Cletus helped ease Mary back down into the chair. They made their way across the small waiting room towards a hallway leading to the hospital proper, away from the emergency area. At the end of the hallway they crossed into the larger hospital entryway. This was a much larger waiting area for guests visiting patients and had a television mounted on a high shelf for visitors to watch while in the waiting area.

As they passed in front of the television, which was showing an early afternoon soap opera, the screen suddenly shifted from a dogfood commercial to a graphic that simply said:

CBS NEWS BULLETIN

A moment later the distinctive voice of Walter Cronkite blared out from the television:

"Here is a bulletin from CBS News. President Kennedy has been the victim of an assassin's bullet in Dallas, Texas. It is not known as yet whether the president survived the attack against him."

~ 50 ~

When Cletus entered Ian's room he appeared to be sleeping. There was a nurse standing by a machine that was monitoring his heart activity and she was looking at the screen on the monitor, transcribing some information to a clipboard that she hung on the foot of the bed as she turned to leave.

Quietly she said, "He's fine. We've put him on a saline drip and given him a mild sedative to control his agitation a little. He may seem to be a little sleepy if you try to speak with him. He may also appear to be a little confused. Don't worry, this is normal."

Cletus thanked her, "Thank you nurse. How is he, really?"

She smiled, "Mr. Armstrong, he's fine. I'm sure you'll be told by the doctors that is was a very mild stroke. It's affected his speech a little, but it seems to be improving. It may be a while before we know if it will return to normal or not. I've seen patients fully recover with much worse effects after a stroke than Mr. MacGregor's, but we'll just have to wait and see how this turns outs. He's in very good health by all other accounts."

Cletus said, "Should I try and talk with him, or not?"

She said, "Let him know you're here. Just don't tire him out too much, okay?" With that, she passed by Cletus leaving him alone with Ian.

Cletus moved a chair to be nearer the head of the bed. As he sat down, Ian opened his eyes and smiled at him.

Cletus moved his hand near Ian's, Ian clasped it, closed his eyes for a moment then opened them and slowly said, "Sorry for all the fuss. Where's Mary?"

Cletus smiled back, "Mary's here, she's fine. Everyone's behind you, it sounds like you had a small stroke. Don't worry about anything, okay?"

Ian nodded.

"Dad, we've got great news. Mary's seen her doctor while she was here. He's going to admit her – her due date is a little closer than he'd predicted …"

Ian made a move to sit up a little but slumped back down onto his pillow. "This didn't … because …"

Cletus cut him off, "Dad it's her time – that's all." He smiled, "It's normal. She'll do okay."

Ian visibly relaxed.

"Mary wanted me come down right away and make sure you were okay and to tell you not to worry about her."

Ian was able to say, "Thank god."

Cletus smiled and said, "Dr. Casey wanted me to tell you that the baby should be arriving in the next day or two and it'll be fine. He thought you'd like to be the first to find out."

Ian now looked to be almost fully awake.

Cletus nodded, "He can clearly hear the heartbeat. They're both fine."

Ian was excited now, "I wish I could see her now."

Cletus said, "She'll probably be down to see you before too much longer. She's going to stay right here at the hospital."

Ian smiled.

Cletus continued, "They're going to keep you here for a little while longer also. Everyone say's this wasn't really very serious. They just want to make sure. Okay?"

Ian nodded.

Cletus got up, "Dad, get some more sleep okay? I'll bring Mary down here in a little while, after Dr. Casey is through."

Ian continued to hold Cletus' hand as Cletus moved from the chair. Ian was trying to speak – Cletus leaned back over Ian – "Tell Katie thanks ...the girl at the pond ...the stone ..." With that he moved his hand away from Cletus', and smiling, closed his eyes and drifted off to sleep.

~ 51 ~

While Mary was being examined by Dr. Casey, Cletus went back to the waiting room and watched what was unfolding in Dallas. Disjointed reports were coming in, but in only a few minutes it was confirmed that President Kennedy had died.

By now, the waiting room was filled with people standing to watch the television. It was unusually quiet, more than a few people were sobbing. Kennedy was so young and energetic. It seemed as though everyone treated his family as their own, following all the antics of his children, mourning when Jackie's newborn son, Patrick, had died in August.

Dr. Casey came out to find Cletus. Mary was fine, but after listening to the baby's heart, he felt she should be admitted. Her due date was not that far off, the stress of Ian's situation had elevated her blood pressure – he just felt that he'd like to keep her in the hospital for closer observation. Cletus thanked him, then pressed him for more information, "You're sure there's nothing seriously wrong with the pregnancy?"

Dr. Casey replied, "Cletus, she's fine, the baby's fine. Really. I want to keep a closer eye on her, that's all. I know her due date is about two weeks away, but sometimes, with a second child, the date may be a little trickier to determine."

Cletus was finally able to relax a little.

Dr. Casey continued, "But I'd like you to come back with me to see Mary. There's something I need to discuss with the two of you."

The two of them pushed their way out of the crowd watching the television, to make their way back to the examination room where Mary was thinking about Ian, her new baby and about Katie and Cletus. She thought about President Kennedy too. Everyone she had encountered was talking about it in hushed tones. When Cletus and the doctor came into the room, she was visibly relieved.

Cletus came to her side, smiling he said, "Mary the doctor says everything is okay, but he wants you to spend the night here, okay? Don't worry about Katie, we've talked about you having to go into the hospital. She'll be fine."

Mary said, "Go back and stay with Dad, okay?"

Cletus smiled, "Sure. He's probably sleeping by now. I'll stay with him if that's what you want."

Mary nodded in agreement.

Dr. Casey stopped Cletus before he left the room. "Don't you want to hear what I wanted to tell the two of you?" he said with a smile.

Cletus said, "Sorry. Please, go ahead."

Dr. Casey said, "Well, it's good news. I won't keep you from Ian. Someone should go back and tell him his two new grandchildren will be fine when they're born in the next day or two."

~ 52 ~

Teddy had gone home to tell Mavis about Ian. He knew she'd want to go the hospital as soon as she found out. Cletus had called Teddy at the course to update him about Ian's condition. Teddy couldn't help but think back to when he'd started at the course. Charles Townsend had met with Teddy and hired him at the end of their discussions about what Teddy would be doing at the course. Teddy had met Ian later that day – it seemed so long ago, and at the same time – it seemed like yesterday. He counted Ian as one of his closest friends – like many others in Jasper.

When he pulled into his driveway there was an unfamiliar car in the driveway. As he walked by it on his way to the side door of the house, he noticed that the license plates were labeled 'US Gov'. When he came through the kitchen towards the living room, two men stood that had been talking with Mavis. Mavis was obviously upset ... "Mr. Tasker, my name is James Reed, and this is David Spencer." He moved forward towards Teddy slightly. "We have some news regarding your daughter Barbara."

Teddy was looking toward Mavis with a questioning look he said, "What's happening?".

Mavis stood, "Teddy. Barbara's gone missing." She had a tissue and brought it up to face.

Reed approached Teddy, "Mr. Tasker, we hope this isn't serious, but Barbara and several other Peace Corps workers are overdue on a return trip to bring supplies back to the hospital they've been working at. They had flown out to the agencies' supply base and were accompanying a small convoy back to their hospital. The convoy is out of communication with the agency. It's been two days ..."

Teddy began, "So you're telling us you have no idea where our daughter is."

Reed began again, "That's correct sir. We have contacted the authorities and they are trying to track the location of the convoy. We may hear from them at any moment. We wanted to apprise you of the situation before any news reports reached you – perhaps misleading you about what is happening."

Mavis came to Teddy's side, "Teddy ..."

Teddy hugged her and led her back to the sofa.

Spencer repositioned himself in a chair next to Teddy. "Mr. Trasker, we're going to do everything it takes to find out what is happening and locate your daughter."

Teddy looked skeptical. "Two days. Our daughter has been missing for two days?"

Spencer nodded yes.

Teddy said to him, "What, exactly, are you doing?"

Reed tried to explain. "Sir, as you know we have military forces in the region as well as civilian personnel investigating what happened. They have received conflicting reports about the last known position of the convoy. They are retracing the route the convoy was supposed to be taking."

All Teddy could say was, "Two days. How many others are with her?"

Reed answered, "The convoy consisted of three vehicles. Seven workers in total."

Spencer added, "Sir, the vehicles were clearly marked as Peace Corps vehicles. No one could mistake them for anything else."

Teddy thanked them for their openness. "Gentlemen, thank you for your efforts. We appreciate your candor."

Spencer continued, "Sir, we're going to stay in Jasper for the next several days. We've left our phone numbers with Mrs. Trasker. If there are any developments, we'll contact you immediately. We'll let ourselves out, I'm sure you need some time to yourselves."

Reed and Spencer moved towards the door with Teddy following close behind. They turned back to face Teddy at the doorway – he shook their hands and thanked them again.

When they'd left, he returned to Mavis. "Mavis, we have to believe that Barb will get through this – she's a smart girl, she knows how to handle herself. Okay? Tell me you agree."

Mavis nodded her head in agreement. "Teddy, our little girl is lost – what is she going through?"

Teddy put his arms around Mavis, "I don't how to answer that – but she'll be okay."

Mavis nodded in agreement.

Teddy said, "I'd like to go see Ian. I won't be long. I thought you'd want to go …but under the circumstances …well I won't be long."

Mavis held Teddy's arm as he started to move away. "I'm going with you. I don't want to stay here by myself. I want to see Ian too."

July 4, 1888

afternoon

On the Fourth of July, Sarah and Josiah hosted an outdoor party for everyone, adjacent to the pond on their farm. Josiah and Tavis had constructed a large table in the shade of the sycamore tree just back from the water's edge. The two families were enjoying food cooked over a pit that had been set up for the occasion.

The weather had stayed warmer than usual, the sky was cloudless, the smoke from the pit was rising perfectly vertical – there was no air movement, which was unusual for the top of Sycamore Hill. Looking across the pond, the house and barn were perfectly mirrored in the water. Overhead, in the sycamore, a blue jay announced his arrival – waiting for the food crumbs that were sure to follow the party.

The meal had finished, and Henry had produced a small keg of hard cider for them to celebrate the occasion. He was in the process of making a toast to also thank the Carson's for joining them at the Glen, when a stranger emerged from the woods along the path from the mill up to the farm. He was tall and in uniform. Dewey turned to see what had stopped Henry's speech. An immediate smile came to his face. He stood and waved to the stranger to join them.

"Captain Fisher! How good of you to join us!" bellowed Dewey, as the man approached the table.

Carlotta stood too, as Henry glanced at the members of the Carson family, he noticed that Sally's complexion had noticeably flushed.

Henry came over to Fisher, "Captain Fisher, I think it was 'Private' Fisher the last time we chatted. Good to see you."

Fisher responded, "Good to see you too Colonel. It's been a fair bit, hasn't it?"

"That is has." Responded Henry. "Please sir, join us – but you have to call me Henry. Let me introduce you to everyone here."

Fisher came over to Carlotta, "Ma'am, nice to see you. I hope you don't mind me joining you here. I've brought some paperwork for the General. I thought if he could take care of it, I could return to Washington and you could enjoy the rest of your furlough as you accompany Miss Carson to Philadelphia."

Carlotta said, "How thoughtful of you Captain. Surly you'll stay over until the General can get through what you've brought?"

Fisher replied, "Yes Ma'am. I've already reserved a room in the hotel."

At that Henry intervened. "Nonsense Captain. You'll stay with us at the Mill. It'll be more convenient – easier to get through your business. Please sit, join us here we've plenty of food. If you've already eaten, join us in some cider from our trees down by the mill."

A knowing smile passed between Carlotta and Dewey, Sally had remained silent – but she too was smiling.

~ 53 ~

When Teddy and Mavis arrived at the hospital, there was a growing contingent of Ian's friends in the waiting area. Most were gathered around the television watching the disjointed reports from Dallas as well as Washington. Air Force One would be landing in Washington soon, it was expected that the new president would speak to the press, to try and assure the nation that the horrific events in Dallas were over – that the nation was safe.

Teddy and Mavis were drawn toward the television. Both had also heard the news but had not watched the television until now. Teddy said to Mavis, "We should have Susan join us. There can't be anybody in MacGregor's with all this going on. We should have her close up so Bruce can go home also."

~ 54 ~

Davis was in MacGregor's with Susan and Chip when the phone behind the bar rang. Bruce was there and answered it. He looked out into the dining area then turned his back on the tables and continued speaking, but in a lower voice.

"I understand Teddy. I'll bring him to the phone. Hold on."

With that, Bruce came out to the booth and said to Chip, "Chip, Teddy's on the phone and says he needs a quick word with you."

Chip stood up, "I'll be right back."

The two of them moved back across the room to the bar. Chip picked up the phone and Bruce moved away, giving him a little privacy to speak with Teddy.

Teddy spoke first, "Chip, you're there with Susan, aren't you?"

Chip was quick with, "Yeah, I'll get her. Just …"

"No!" was Teddy's quick response.

Chip turned his back on the room, "Teddy, what's happening?"

Teddy said, "I'd like you and Susan to come down to the hospital. We came down to look in on Ian, but we need to talk to you and Susan. Is Davis there?"

"Yes Teddy, he's with us here in the tavern. Why do you need to see us?"

Teddy said, "I'll explain when you get here. You should bring Davis along also. Don't get anyone worked up, or anything. I'm sure we can find a quiet spot here to talk."

"Teddy, I don't understand"

Teddy said, "There's something happening that may involve Barbara. We don't have a lot of information, but I need to speak with all of you about it. Please come down here. Just try not to alarm Susan or Davis. I appreciate you handling this Chip."

Chip responded, "We'll leave now and should be there shortly."

Teddy said, "Please take your time, drive safely coming down off the hill. Thanks."

Teddy hung up, as did Chip. He turned and made his way back to the table.

His words with Teddy must have had a noticeable effect on him, Susan asked if he was okay. "Chip, what's happening? Is everything okay?"

Chip mustered up a smile. "Teddy would like us to come down to the hospital. You too, Davis."

Susan's complexion started to change – she was becoming really nervous.

Chip continued, "Ian's okay. He's doing fine. So is Mary. He didn't want to panic us, but he'd like for us to join them at the hospital. He said he'd explain when we got there."

Susan went to the bar and explained to Bruce that she had to leave. Bruce said that he'd handle everything at MacGregor's. It was getting late in the afternoon. There wouldn't be much business now until the Friday evening dinner crowd. Teddy had suggested he close up MacGregor's and asked that he have Curtis close the course as well. Since they had been watching the television and seeing the events unfold in Dallas, not a single customer had come in. Most had left after seeing the reports on the television. He told Susan that if no one came in by five he'd probably close for the evening, she agreed.

~ 55 ~

When Susan and the others arrived at the hospital, Teddy and Mavis were waiting for them in the reception area. It was still crowded with people staring at the television. He guided them over to the far side of the room, few people were nearby. Teddy motioned for them to sit.

Teddy started to speak but was interrupted by Susan.

"Somethings happened to Barbara …" she said. Not a question, but a statement.

Teddy nodded and tried to speak again.

Susan said, "Don't worry, she's okay." she said with a forced smile.

This did bring a slight smile to his face. He said, "Is there anything else I need to know?"

"Please Dad, I'm sorry …"

Teddy said, "That's okay." He paused for a moment, "A convoy of Peace Corps supply vehicles that Barbara is on is overdue. We don't have a lot of details, but searchers have been sent out to retrace their route."

Mavis had been silent, but Susan had immediately sensed this and was sitting beside her.

Chip said, "Do we know when they'll have more information?"

Teddy explained, "Two men from the agency visited us to tell us what was happening. They will be staying over for several days, so when more information is available, they'll keep us updated."

Davis hadn't said anything. Obviously, he too was upset. Finally, he said, "Do we know where she left from on the convoy?"

"Saigon." was all Teddy said.

He looked up to see Reed and Spencer entering the room. Seeing Teddy, they came directly over to him. Teddy stood - there was a pause as Reed said, "Sir we returned to our motel and there was a message waiting for us. Mrs. Trasker mentioned that a friend had been hospitalized, so we came here when there was no answer on your home phone."

Mavis grasped Teddy's hand.

"Your daughter is okay." Said Reed.

Spencer was watching closely, Reed turned to look at him. He had to step away from Teddy and Mavis.

Teddy looked anxiously at Spencer.

Spencer said, "I don't know how to explain this. Everyone was set free – except Barbara. Apparently, she asked that everyone be let go. In exchange …she offered to go with her captors to help in a facility that they were stealing the medical supplies for."

Reed had collected himself, "As you can imagine the captives are distraught over this. To a person, they wanted to stay with Barbara. She convinced the captors that she was the most useful one on the convoy, and that the rest would be a burden – she wanted to help."

Mavis was quietly sobbing, Teddy tried to hold tears back but couldn't. "That is Barbara …she knows how to take care of herself."

"Sir," began Spencer, "We have troops out now looking for her."

Teddy said, "I sense there's a 'But' coming next."

"Sir," said Spenser, "The area this occurred in is just about the worst spot for us to try and search. I know it seems that since it's so close to Saigon you might believe it is somehow 'safer'. But it's not.

It's rumored that these people have even gone underground to avoid detection. Many of the local villagers support these guerilla fighters. It's very difficult to gather any information in this region."

Teddy didn't know what to say next.

Davis stood to address Spencer, "But she's not injured?"

Spencer answered, "No sir. No one was seriously injured. Only the driver of one of the vehicles was injured. He had some bruises from a scuffle when they were captured.

~ 56 ~

Cletus and Mary were finally able to join Ian in his room. He appeared to be sleeping when they entered but opened his eyes immediately as they came closer to his bed.

Mary put her hand up against her father's face. "Dad, how are you doing?"

Ian nodded, "Good, I'm fine." He spoke slowly but his speech had improved a little.

Mary's demeanor improved visibly, she smiled.

"Question is – how are you doing?" Ian said.

She put her hand on her abdomen, "We're doing fine, all of us."

Cletus smiled now as Ian looked at him also. "Not me, I'm a wreck." He said.

Ian looked confused. He turned to face Mary.

"Twins." Was all she said as she lightly patted her tummy.

A tear come down Ian's cheek, he grasped Mary's hand and squeezed it. Smiling, he dozed off.

July 4, 1888

evening

After dark, the women had retreated to the kitchen in the nearby farmhouse, while the men disassembled the picnic table. This was the excuse for them to linger around the fire as the darkness first deepened and then brightened as an early moon began to rise.

Close to the water, Tavis and Fisher were talking about Fishers' adventures in the west. Henry and Dewey were near the fire. There was still some cider left in the keg – but not much, soon it would be empty.

Dewey said, "Henry, it doesn't seem so long ago now does it?"

Henry chuckled, "Not that long at all."

Dewey continued, "Henry, why'd you really leave the army?"

Henry thought for a moment, "Everyone thought I was good at it – you know - the killing. I think I was maybe a little better than just *good* at it."

Dewey pushed some coals around in the fire, giving Henry some time to continue.

Henry took a deep breath, in a somewhat halting voice said, "Problem is – I loved it."

Tavis and Fisher had come nearer the fire and stared into it. They had heard the soft tones of Henry's voice, the raw emotion.

Henry and Dewey didn't notice them as they approached, both were also staring into the fire.

Henry continued, "Maybe you understand, maybe not. You're my best friend, we went through a lot and I know you're an exceptional soldier. I know you've killed a lot of people in the course of your career – but you're not really a killer, not like me."

Tavis looked at Henry than Dewey. Dewey was nodding his head.

Henry went on, "Anyway, that's why I got out of the army. It's why I don't want no statue. Not for that. The other boys that left here to fight – some of them never came back – they're the ones that deserve a statue – not me. I don't want any part of it.!"

Tavis saw the determination in Henry's face, saw the darkness in Henry's brown eyes. He and Henry had discussed this several times. Not too long ago it had been the topic of discussion on the long wagon ride to the distant village of Bingley. After listening to Henry's arguments about not wanting a statue, Tavis finally agreed to do whatever he could, if Henry were to die, to prevent a monument being placed on his grave. A simple stone was fine with Henry. He had made it well known that he didn't want any part of a statue or any other honors.

Henry just hoped that Tavis would be able to help if circumstances changed after his death.

~ 57 ~

The week after Thanksgiving was normally a busy week at Sycamore Glen. Golfers would try to get in one final round of golf before the course closed and the season was over. It was different this year. Everyone was absorbed with the death of President Kennedy. No one had shown up to play at the start of the week, so Dan decided to close the course. The office area needed to be moved so the MacGregor's kitchen could be reconstructed. The turmoil was expected, but everything at the course seemed to be out of balance.

Ian had been released from the hospital, but it was decided that he should stay with Cletus and Mary for a while. He said he'd be fine in his apartment, but Mary wasn't listening to him. She wanted him close by.

She had also returned from the hospital – with two new daughters. Mary and Cletus had decided to name them Sara and Ruth. The names had appealed to them during the course of the summer with all the discussion about Henry.

The house atop Sycamore Hill was a hub of activity as people stopped in to see Ian, the babies and Mary.

Claire and Dan had stopped in on Thursday - bringing the Judge with them to visit Ian. Claire was busy in the kitchen preparing a meal for everyone. Mary was helping, but Claire kept shushing her out of the kitchen into the dining room – to sit.

Ian's voice was practically normal – he just had to take a little more time when speaking. Although he was frustrated at times, he was adapting. Dan and Cletus were with him in the living room, Katie was playing in her room.

Dan was explaining to Ian what he and Claire thought about Clarissa – who her father was.

"So, you think this whole thing hinges on the color of her eyes?" asked Ian.

Dan explained what Claire had learned. "Yup, Claire's been digging into this and there's basically no way that Jedidiah could have been Clarissa's father based on the genes it would take to produce brown eyes."

Cletus asked, "When was Clarissa born? Do we have her exact birthdate?"

The Judge answered, "1862. I'm not certain of the exact date. I think it was in the spring."

Dan got up and went into the kitchen. "Claire what was Clarissa's birthdate? Do you remember?"

Claire thought for a while, "Sometime in January 1862, I think. Why"

"Cletus asked, we're just doing a little exercise." Dan replied.

"April 1861" said Claire. "I think I know where you're headed with this."

"Of course, you do." Said Dan, smiling, as he left and went back into the living room.

When Dan gave Cletus the date, Cletus sat back in his chair mulling over the dates. Finally, he said, "Let's assume that Jedidiah is not Clarissa's father because of the eye color. This means someone else would have had relations with Ruth at about the same time Jedidiah and Henry left for the war."

The Judge had drifted away from the conversation about Clarissa's age. He was deep in thought. But when her name was mentioned again by Cletus he blurted out – "It was lighter."

Dan stared as the Judge; Claire came out of the kitchen.

The Judge continued, "That box was lighter when I stuffed it into Clarissa's bag than what we removed from the safety deposit box!"

The Judge hesitated. He was thinking back fifty years.

Cletus urged him on. "Go on."

The Judge added, "I couldn't put my finger on it until just now. Clarissa added the Diary. I never handled the Time Capsule. Clarissa had it in her bag when we took it to the bank later that week. I never touched it again until Claire opened it."

Cletus said to Claire, "Whose name is in the diary?"

Claire hesitated. No one had asked – yet. Everyone assumed it was Henry's wife Ruth's diary. But the fact was there was no name in it. She finally had to tell everyone. "There's no name in it." She said.

Dan said, "No name?"

"No," said Claire. "No name - and the first page is missing – it's been very neatly cut out."

July 5, 1888

The next morning, after everyone had eaten breakfast, Henry took Fisher down into the mill room to explain the operation of the mill. Dewey was busy with the paperwork that Fisher had brought with him and would be occupied with it most of the day. Ruth and Carlotta were in the kitchen with Clarissa and Sally, preparing to bake bread for the week since all the bread had been used up during the big meal the day before. Ruth suggested to Clarissa that she take Sally out on one of the trails through the woods and show her more of Sycamore Hill.

Clarissa asked Sally, "Do you have any riding clothes? If you don't, I'm sure some of mine will fit."

Sally responded, "I have some, but I didn't unpack them. Would you mind if I borrowed some of your items?"

Clarissa said, "Come on, we'll find something for you. My feet look a little bigger than yours, but it'll be okay – you don't want to ruin a pair of shoes, I'm sure a pair of my boots will fit."

As the two of them stalked off towards Clarissa's room, Carlotta smiled. "I wish Sally had had a sister to grow up with." She said to Ruth.

There was a sadness in Ruth as she nodded and said wistfully, "I know what you mean. It's been tough on Clarissa, but Mary is close by – they're practically sisters."

Carlotta continued, "It must have been wonderful for you growing up with a twin, especially one as nice as Sarah."

Ruth was smiling broadly and quietly agreed, "You have no idea."

~

Henry and Fisher were beneath the stones in the mill. Henry was explaining how the stones needed to be swapped out when the grooves in each stone became worn and ineffective. Fisher looked up at the bedstone.

"You don't think of the stones being that big until you stand this close to them, do you?" he said.

Henry agreed, "They are a lot heavier and dangerous than they look from a distance."

Fisher walked to the stones laying against the nearby wall. He couldn't help but touch them and push against them to sense the mass of the stones.

Henry watched him, "Do you really want to get a sense of the weight of these stones?"

Fisher said, "What do you have in mind?"

"Help me swap out this set. They're about due for reworking. If I get them recut now - they'll be sharp and ready for the fall."

"Just show me how I can help." Said Fisher.

"Well, we have to go upstairs and move the running stone away from the bedstone first." Said Henry. "Then we have to use the equipment to lower the bedstone down to the floor, then lower the running stone down here also."

The two of them climbed the nearby stairs and Fisher watched as Henry disengaged the gear of the mill from the running stone. When the gear was clear, he moved the hoist and grapple into position over the stones. He proceeded to hook the grapple into the two pockets on the edge of the running stone which allowed him to lift it clear of the bedstone. Fisher helped Henry swing the stone away towards the nearby outside wall – Henry carefully lowered the stone to the floor.

Henry then repositioned the grapple over the bedstone. He hooked it into the pockets of the bedstone and lifted it off the bedstone risers that controlled its position to the running stone.

Henry raised the stone and when it was high enough, he pivoted it on the grapple hooks so it could pass through the floor 'on edge' diagonally through the opening.

At this point he tied it off to hold it in place and returned to the basement. He would guide the stone through the opening while Fisher lowered the stone from above.

Henry was standing beneath the stone, guiding it through the hole when the grapple slipped, and the stone came free of it on one side. The stone smashed through the leveling support angle and crossbeam as it crashed down into the basement.

Fisher ran down the stairs to find Henry on the floor with the stone laying on top of him. The edge of the stone had caught him fully across his chest as the stone toppled sideways when hitting the floor.

Instinctively Fisher tried to lift the stone with his bare hands. It wouldn't budge. Henry was conscious, but unable to move or speak with the crushing weight on his chest – his pleading eyes fixed on Fisher trying to move the stone. As Fisher looked at Henry, Henry's eyes shifted to the side several times. Fisher looked in that direction and saw the pry bar.

He grabbed it and was able to shift the stone – Henry was unable to move very much. Fisher yelled for help. No one had come yet – the falling stone had not made much noise.

Fisher repositioned the bar several times by sliding the bar on the floor without lifting it as much.

Finally, he had it far enough where he felt he could both lift and push the stone sideways. If fell with a thump next to Henry.

Henry was still not moving much; he was trying to take a full breath – but couldn't – obviously it was too painful.

Fisher bent low over Henry – he was trying to speak.

"Sara …" was all he could get out.

Fisher responded, "I'll get Ruth, she'll send for Sara."

"Sara." Henry repeated, he was close to losing consciousness.

Fisher said to him, "I have to leave for a moment, I'll be right back. Don't try to move!"

Fisher bolted out of the room, racing out the door, he had to run the length of the mill to reenter the kitchen door. Ruth and Carlotta were there sitting at the kitchen table – startled when the door flew open.

"Henry's hurt bad. He's calling for Sara." Fisher blurted out.

Ruth and Carlotta were up out of their chairs, running, following Fisher back to Henry.

Henry's eyes were closed when they reached him. Ruth screamed out, "Henry!"

Henry partially opened his eyes. He was breathing slightly now, but blood was trickling out of the corner of his mouth. The shallow breaths he was taking were obviously painful to take.

"Sara …", he managed to say.

Fisher told him, "I'm going to go get her. Stay still, we'll get a doctor."

Henry tried to shake his head 'no' but, could only move it slightly. As Fisher stood to leave, Ruth grabbed his arm, "Henry I'm here." She said.

Henry slowly nodded his head. He had taken several shallow breaths, enough to be able to say, "I know you are." He gave a small cough, then took a couple of small breaths. Then struggled to say, "I've known all along."

Fisher looked at Charlotte, questioning her with his eyes.

After a couple more breaths Henry said, "I've known about Clarissa … from the start."

Ruth was crying. Nodding, she said, "We should have told you – we couldn't"

"Under...stand." Henry rasped out.

Fisher said, "Ruth – I've got to get a doctor. Carlotta can go get Sara."

Ruth shook her head, "Peter please go for the doctor. I want Carlotta to stay with me."

Fisher said, "You're sure?"

"Yes." Said Ruth.

Fisher ran from the mill.

Carlotta moved closer to Henry and Ruth.

"Sara ... I'm sorry." Henry struggled to say.

Ruth said, "You have nothing to be sorry about. You've given us a wonderful daughter and made a good home for us."

"Loved you since ... first saw you." Henry said before coughing more blood. Grimacing, he took several more shallow breaths.

"And I loved you since you wandered into my life with Jack. I think Ruth did too in her own way." Said Sara.

Carlotta looked at her, then Henry.

"Carlotta, I'm Sara," she said. "When I was pregnant with Henry's daughter, Ruth and I switched ... lives. It would have been impossible raising Clarissa – being unmarried."

Henry managed a smile, "My eyes."

Sara smiled, "Yes, Clarissa has your eyes."

"Your heart." Said Henry

"Don't talk too much. Peter's getting a doctor", Sara said.

Henry slowly shook his head, "Keep the secret."

Tears were rolling down Sara's cheeks now.

Henry labored heavily to take several breaths, "She won't understand ... hate us for this."

Sara nodded again. Tears were streaming down her cheeks.

The door burst open, Clarissa and Sally came in. Clarissa rushed to Henry's side. She took his hand., Henry opened his eyes.

His breathing was slowing down, more blood coming from his mouth. He managed a small cough – to speak, "Clarissa my …"

As his eyes fluttered for a moment, Clarissa cried out "Father!"

"Yes." Was all Henry could manage as his eyes closed. His struggle was over.

Steven Wainwright had thought about this for some time. All through the fall he wondered if he should say anything to the Judge or to Claire. Finally, he made up his mind and picked the telephone up to call the Mayor.

"Madam Mayor," he began. "This is Steven at the bank."

"Steven, how nice to hear from you. "How can I help you?" Claire responded.

"Mayor …", he started again.

"Steven – please …" responded Claire.

"Claire – I'd like to discuss something with you. Do you have some time today when we could meet?"

"Steven, it's nearly noon. Do you have anything planned for lunch? We could meet at Johnnies – unless you need me to come into your office."

Steven replied, "That would be fine Claire. Shall we say 12:30?"

"Perfect.", said Claire. "I'll be there then."

Claire finished her work not long after Steven's call. She closed up her office and walked across the village green to her home. She wanted to freshen up before her lunch date with Steven. On her way out the door she left a note for Dan that she would be at Johnnies for a business lunch and that she would see him later.

Not trusting the weather, she drove to Johnnies and parked along the curb in front of the restaurant. When she entered, she was greeted by Nancy.

"Claire, how nice to see you. Steven called to reserve a booth. He's not here yet, but I'll show you to your table."

"Thank you, Nancy," said Claire. "Have you finished up your holiday shopping yet?"

"No," replied Nancy. "How about you?"

"No," replied Claire. "Almost, but there's still a couple items I need to get."

"Can I get you something to drink?" Asked Nancy.

"How about a cup of tea. It's getting colder out there now." Answered Claire.

As Nancy left the table, she passed Steven coming into the dining area. He thanked her as she nodded back toward the corner of the dining room where Claire was seated.

"Afternoon Mayor." Said Steven as he sat at the table.

"Really Steven." Was Claire's response.

Steven chuckled, then relented – "Nice to see you Claire. Thanks for meeting on such short notice."

Nancy returned with Claire's tea and asked Steven if he'd like something to drink. "Would you care for something to drink?" she asked as she laid menus down in front of Claire and Steven.

"Just a coffee Nancy. Thanks." He replied.

Claire began looking the menu over, but after several moments she laid it down after noticing Steven was making no attempt at ordering a meal. He was fidgeting, obviously his mind was not on having lunch.

"Steven, what's on your mind?" she finally asked.

"I'm not sure you can help, but I can't think of any other way …" he began.

Claire patiently looked at him.

"Claire as president of the bank I'm entrusted with all manner of transactions. We safeguard many things. We're bound by regulations in almost all circumstances." He hesitated before continuing.

"This may be one of those times the rules don't help me much."

"Steven, start from the beginning." Said Claire.

Nancy approached the table and sat Steven's coffee in from of him. "Would you like to order now?" she asked.

Claire said, "I'd like a salad and a bowl of the French onion soup please."

Nancy turned toward Steven, "Just a salad for me Nancy. Thanks."

Nancy left to get their meals.

Steven took a quick sip of his coffee. He leaned back in the booth against the back of his seat. "Have you ever heard of the term 'escheatment'?" he asked.

Claire thought for a moment and answered, "No."

"Well it's the term we use when a customers' account has been inactive for a long period of time – at which point we are required to report the account as 'abandoned' to the government."

"So, this involves an inactive bank account?" asked Claire.

"Not really." Said Steven. "It's about an inactive safety deposit box."

This got Claire's attention. "A safety deposit box?"

"Well the term applies to unclaimed 'property' which in this case is a safety deposit box at the bank."

"So, you're referring to the safety deposit box of the Judges that we opened this summer?" asked Claire.

Steven hesitated. "No this is another box." He said.

Claire was puzzled. "Another box? I don't understand."

Steven continued, "The owner of the box that you and the Judge opened – owned a second box."

Claire had lost any interest in her meal that Nancy was bringing. She barely acknowledged that it had been delivered.

"The thing is," explained Steven, "these boxes were not rented, they were purchased."

Claire said, "Isn't that unusual? I mean, I have a box that I pay a yearly rental fee on. I didn't know that I could purchase a box."

Steven agreed. "I know this is unusual. But at the time it was part of a promotion. The bank must have felt it was a way to bring in customers. In looking back through the safety deposit box records, it doesn't appear that many boxes were being rented out at that time."

Claire said, "I just assumed the Judge was paying the rental on the box."

"No." said Steven."

Claire was stunned. "Can you tell me who purchased the box?"

Steven answered, "Mrs. C. Osborne. Clarissa – your grandmother."

Claire thought for a moment. Steven could see the puzzled look on her face.

"Claire, the problem is there is a codicil as a part of the purchase of the boxes. She stated that the ownership of the boxes were to be kept 'private'."

Claire was thinking about it, Steven added, "That's my problem. I have to keep the terms intact, but I feel the property is now 'inactive' in the eyes of the law."

"Claire, I've spoken with the judge a little – about the box being opened. I understand there's some confusion regarding who Henry was married to …"

Claire nodded, "Yes we think we have it all sorted out."

"Good." Said Steven. "There may be nothing to this second box – I'm just trying to follow the law."

Claire said, "I appreciate your concern Steven. Perhaps this second box will help clear up the confusion that the Judge spoke of."

"Well he explained some of it to me Claire, and I don't mean to pry, but I don't want to affect the Judge's health. He seems so fragile Claire."

"Well he does seem to have slipped back into poorer health Steven, but he's still mentally very sharp. Perhaps with some more information to process about all this he'll bounce back a little."

Steven went on to explain how the box would be opened. "So, Claire – since there does not seem to be a key for the box, we'll need to drill the lock. I'll arrange for that. I'm going to transfer ownership to you. If you'll come in and witness the opening of the box that will satisfy my obligations on behalf of the bank. I think I can explain enough of this to the examiner to avoid any problems.

Nancy came up to the table. "I hope your meals are okay. It looks as though you two forgot all about eating."

Claire laughed, "Sorry Nancy but we just got lost in conversation."

Nancy said, "Well I'm going to get you another bowl of soup. I'll be right back." She retrieved Claire's soup and left for the kitchen.

"Sorry Claire. I didn't mean to spoil your lunch." Said Steven.

Claire put her hand on his, "Don't worry about it. I'm not terribly hungry. Finding out about this second box is much more important to me."

"Well I'm just glad this is settled. It has bothered me for quite some time. I actually have an appetite." He said as he dove into his salad.

Claire said, "Maybe this will clear up some Sycamore Glen secrets."

July 8, 1888

Henry's funeral was held on Sunday, July 8. No one knew exactly where Henry was from – nobody from outside Jasper attended. His shocking death affected the entire community.

'Sara' and Josiah asked that Henry's funeral service be held at the farm. 'Ruth' agreed. The mill had shut down and wouldn't reopen for some time.

Dewey asked if he could speak at the funeral, 'Ruth' agreed.

The day was warm, the sky cloudless. It was decided to hold the funeral outdoors since so many people would be attending. 'Ruth' was numb, her movements mechanical. Clarissa was hit the hardest. She had barely spoken to anybody.

When Dewey rose to speak, all the politely, soft spoken, conversations taking place amongst those attending the funeral stopped.

"I see before me everyone that mattered most to Henry. I know he came to this community looking for work – but what he found was a new life. I'm sure each of you has a story to tell about how you met him. I haven't had the opportunity to get to know most of you in the short time that my family and I have been here. But I'd like you to hear about how I met Henry.

I was a teenager off to fight in a war that I thought would be a big adventure. I thought I knew all that I needed to be a soldier. I was wrong. Sergeant Hawkins was a tough ... well let's just leave it at that. Even at that point he was a person that was listened to when he spoke. He tried to pass on all he knew about surviving. I listened, I'm sure that's why I'm here today. Many more men will tell you the same story.

I've stayed in the army and seen many soldiers perform – but I've never met anyone as proficient and professional as Henry Hawkins. As a marksman, he is without doubt the finest I've ever seen. He tried to pass the same knowledge on to me, and while I improved, I came nowhere near his excellence.

Only on rare occasions did I ever hear Henry talk about 'home'. He would tell us to forget about the past and the future – stay in the moment – survive. But when he talked of 'home', it was about the beauty of the Glen – about the friendliness of the people here – about it being his 'home'. I asked him if there was anyone special waiting for him and he would be vague, but I always knew there was 'someone' here. Having finally met his family I can see how hard it must have been for him to leave all that behind. In the short time we've been here now, I can see how special Henry has been to all of you. In such a tight knit community, I'm sure that Henry was someone you could all rely on when needed.

At Cedar Creek, where Henry was wounded, he was standing amidst a grove of Sycamore trees almost as majestic as these here in the Glen. As we retreated, we sought shelter in the trees, they protected us – perhaps saving our lives.

Earlier this week Henry brought me up through the glen to the pond out here behind us. I had a sense of the security and belonging that I think Henry must have felt – here at 'home'.

There was a smattering of quiet applause as Dewey moved back towards Carlotta and Sally.

The minister closed the service with a prayer and the gathering broke up. Most would accompany the casket down the hill to the village cemetery.

Later in the afternoon the families and their guests were back at the farm. There were several groups of friends scattered about – talking of Henry.

Dewey, Fisher and Tavis had walked across to the far side of the pond and stood under the sycamore, near the millstone. Fisher was struggling with what he had been a part of.

"Sir," he said, "I feel responsible. It happened so fast – if I had reacted quicker, I know he wouldn't have been injured so badly."

"Peter," Dewey responded, "None of this was your fault. Everyone is grateful for you helping the way you did. I know Ruth and Clarissa are glad to have been with him at the end."

Tavis felt the same, "Peter, it was an accident – that's all. Henry and I should have improved that whole grapple arrangement. If we had – maybe this wouldn't have happened."

Dewey said, "I'm going back to the house. Peter don't let this eat you up."

"I won't sir." Was his response.

"Peter," began Dewey.

"Sir?" responded Fisher.

"Why don't we just use 'Dewey' and 'Peter', okay?" said Dewey.

"Yes sir," said Fisher.

Dewey chuckled, putting his head down he walked slowly away making his way around the pond back towards the farmhouse.

Fisher and Tavis had remained quiet for a while. Finally, Fisher said to Tavis, "Did you know about Sara ... and Ruth?"

Tavis said to him, "How do you mean?"

Fisher silently stared at Tavis.

Tavis quietly said, "Yes."

"How?", asked Fisher.

Tavis said, "Henry figured everything out based on Clarissa's eyes. I mean she really does bear a resemblance to Henry, but – the unusual dark brown eyes ..."

Fisher agreed, "Clarissa does seem to have unusually dark brown eyes – similar to Henry's."

Tavis went on, "He needed someone to talk to about it. We had no secrets. He figured they thought it was easier to switch names between Sara and Ruth than face the shame of the community for having a child out of wedlock. I never met Jedidiah, but I've seen the picture – the color of his eyes."

Fisher said, "It must have been so difficult for them – and she never told Henry?"

Tavis said, "No, according to Henry – no. I imagine Sara and Ruth must have just agreed to a complete – lie."

Fisher said, "What about Josiah?"

Tavis shook his head, "I don't think so. He and Henry have always been close, but no, I don't think Henry said anything to him. He might still know though."

Well," said Fisher, "The secret is safe with me."

Tavis agreed, "Same with me. I care for everyone here …"

Fisher smiled, "I know. If you don't mind me saying, it's pretty obvious – I mean you and Mary."

Tavis was now smiling also. "It's that obvious?"

"Yes." Was all Fisher answered.

Tavis said, "Well sir I think I've seen the same thing between you and Miss Carson."

Fisher laughed, "Well, I'm a lot older than Miss Carson …"

"I don't think age has anything to do with it." Said Tavis.

"Perhaps,'" said Fisher, "but I don't know how the General and Mrs. Carson would feel about it."

"I'm a simple man," said Tavis, "but I know love when I see it – and so do they. I think they're already treating you like the son they know you'll become in the future."

"Maybe …," said Fisher, "but before I pursue Miss Carson, I want to give her a chance for school."

"You see," said Tavis, "that's why I know you're the perfect mate for Sally. She lights up whenever you're around. And I'd guess that Mrs. Carson can attest that a little difference in age shouldn't keep two people apart."

"True." Said Fisher.

"I know the General has talked a little of retiring. What about you? What happens if he decides to retire?" asked Tavis.

Fisher replied, "I don't know how serious he is, or when he'll really decide to retire – but I think if he leaves the army, so will I."

"Because of Sally?" Tavis asked.

"Yes." Replied Fisher. He looked up into the sky and studied the clouds for several minutes.

"Think I'll head back and see if I can help with anything over there" He said pointing toward the farmhouse. Several clusters of people could be seen scattered about.

Tavis just nodded silently but remained standing under the sycamore. He stared up into the towering tree. He thought of Henry's demand that no monument be erected over his grave. Tavis smiled – he had the solution – if need be. Then he stared down at the single mill stone.

'Perhaps Jack wouldn't be alone anymore …if need be.' He thought.

~ 59 ~

It was Christmas morning; Davis had laid in bed all night without sleeping. Finally, near dawn, he knew what he had to do. He had planned on calling his parents later in the day. He waited until he knew that they would be up and called. After chatting with his mother, he asked her to put his father on the phone. When his father took the phone and began talking about what he'd been doing recently, Davis patiently listened and tried his best to carry on a normal conversation – but his father knew something was bothering him. Finally, he quietly said to him, "Son, what's bothering you. You don't sound like your usual self."

Davis began, he related the events surrounding Barbara's disappearance. "Dad let's keep this between the two of us for the time being. Okay?" His father agreed. Then Davis asked him for a favor.

"Dad, I need you to speak with an old friend of yours."

His father knew what was coming next. He didn't like it. "Son I think I know what you're going to ask me to do …"

"Dad I have to go. It's just that simple. The Admiral can recommend me for a position - that'll help. I have to do what I can."

His father said, "I know. I know you. I know what you're made of. I also know I can't stop you once your mind is made up." There was a tear forming in the corner of his eye, but there was a smile forming on his face as he slowly nodded. He was proud of his son, he always was – and always would be.

There was silence between them.

Finally, Davis said, "I'm going, either way. This way's better. I'm also going to need you to help Mom understand this, once I get everything arranged."

Their conversation continued for a while. Finally, they said their goodbyes and the call ended.

Davis' father continued to stay seated at his desk by the phone. He looked out at the fluffy snowflakes slowly drifting downwards just outside the nearby window. It all looked so quiet and peaceful – the snow draped out across everything as far as he could see. As the sun rose higher, the snow crystals began sparkling. The snowfall wasn't intense, just enough to hold your attention on individual flakes as they dropped past the window.

There was a sound from elsewhere in the house that snapped him out of his reverie of the snow – bringing him back into the present.

His wife came into the room and saw him staring out the window.

~

After a long discussion she had left the room retreating to the kitchen. He looked back out the window. The sky had darkened, the snow was falling so heavily now that it was blocking the sun.

When she returned several minutes later, she was carrying a cup of hot chocolate for him. She studied him as he continued to stare at the snow falling.

"I remember when he and those Mapstone kids that lived next door would have snowball fights in weather like this." She said.

"And you would always have a cup of hot chocolate ready for him when he came back in." He said as tears came down across his cheeks.

He turned and reached for the phone.

~ Epilogue ~

Not all the battle reports that were filed after the Allied struggle to secure a beachhead at Anzio during World War II found their way into the official accounts of the battle. Some of them would later be recovered, but the rest didn't exist in any usable form. Maybe in the future, historians would sort it all out.

If they had been found intact, they would have included a report about a young sergeant named Steele that had selflessly thrown himself on a grenade to save the other members of his platoon that were pinned down on the beachhead. But the grenade never exploded. Those around him would never forget his bravery, his heroism.

By the time the platoon had fought its way across Europe and into Germany, the sergeant, who was now a lieutenant, was the sole survivor of that platoon that had entered the war at Anzio.

So, history would forget his heroic act.

Perhaps a better definition of heroism, is bravery and survival under extreme conditions, and maybe the lack of evidence to support any other conclusion.

People need heroes. When one doesn't exist …they invent one.

~ Characters ~

Characters introduced in Sycamore Glen:
Cletus Armstrong – grounds manager of Sycamore Glen
Mary Armstrong – married to Cletus, daughter of Ian MacGregor
Katie Armstrong – daughter of Mary and Cletus
Ian MacGregor – owner of MacGregor's Pub
Dan Steele – majority owner of Sycamore Glen
Claire Osborn Townsend Steele – married to Dan Steele
Henry Osborn - retired Judge – Claire's father
Curtis Aldridge – Sycamore Glen clubhouse manager
Steve "Teddy" Trasker – director of operations Sycamore Glen
Mavis Trasker – married to Teddy
Barbara Trasker – twin daughter of Teddy, college student
Susan Trasker – twin daughter of Teddy, works at MacGregor's

Characters introduced in Sycamore Mill:
Chip Connors – Cabinetmaker
Dick Taylor - Homebuilder
Phil Jackson - Mason
Davis Templeton – teaching Pro at Sycamore Glen
Dr. Casey
Peter Fisher Jr. – visitor to Sycamore Glen
Steven Wainwright – Bank manager

Sycamore Mill ~ 1863:
Henry Hawkins – farmer
Jack – Henrys mule
Ralph Bartlett – Dry Goods Store owner
Ezekiel Jennings – Farmer
Mary Stewart Jennings – Ezekiel's wife
Chastity Ruth Jennings – twin daughter of Ezekiel
Grace Sarah Jennings – twin daughter of Ezekiel
Jedidiah Prescott – married to Ruth Jennings
Clarissa Prescott – daughter of Ruth
Isaac Mueller – owner of Sycamore Glen Mill
Josiah Mueller – married to Sarah Jennings
Mary Mueller – daughter of Sarah

Tavis McDonald – married to Mary Mueller
Wilbur Osborn – married to Clarissa Prescott
Dewey Carson – solider, friend of Henry Hawkins
Carlotta Carson – wife of Dewey
Sally Carson – daughter of Dewey
Peter Fisher – soldier, marries Sally Carson
Jimmy Greaves – rebel soldier

~ Afterword ~

In writing Sycamore Mill as a follow up effort to my first novel, Sycamore Glen, I've placed several characters in the military during the Civil War. My intention is not to try to write an in-depth novel about the Civil War. Other authors ahead of me have written many fine books about the war. My use of the Civil War as a backdrop for the community of Jasper, and how it affects those who fought in the war, is just a device to explore how individuals react to war. The soldiers that fought on both sides may have entered the war for a variety of reasons. I believe that each of them, probably had cause to re-examine their purpose in the war on more than a few occasions. Each was tested. How the war changed their lives and their communities in the aftermath, and far into the future, was one of the goals in this effort. I needed situations that occur in war to reveal the depth of the characters in the story.

While I was working on Sycamore Glen, I really did not think I would do any other writing. By the time I had finished, and others had read my material, my plans changed. One of the first readers of the Sycamore Glen manuscript suggested I write a Civil War story - at about the same time my wife suggested I write a trilogy of stories about Sycamore Glen. Apparently romance novelists tend to write books in trilogies to complete their involvement with sets of characters that might not be possible in a single novel.

Brad G. Leech

Sycamore Secrets

What follows is a sample from the final installment of the Sycamore Glen trilogy, the sequel to Sycamore Mill:

(South Vietnam – Late, 1967)

The helicopter co-pilot looked at his watch trying not to be too obvious about it. He glanced at the fuel gauge - did the math in his head. This time he said something about it.

"Smitty we're 40 clicks out, fuel is bingo in 20 minutes." As he said the words, the 20-minute warning light came on.

The pilot glanced at him momentarily then continued looking out past the skid on his side, forward into the endless sea of elephant grass that bordered the thicker, jungle vegetation. "Roger that." He replied. He looked back briefly at the crew chief and simultaneously the two of them, and the door gunner, began singing. "B–I–N–G–O … B–I–N–G–O… B-I-N–G–O … and Bingo was his name-o."

"Smitty, all I'm saying is …bingo in … 18 minutes." The co-pilot said glancing at his watch again.

"Don't worry, all we got'ta do is pull in somewhere and fill 'er up." He responded. "It ain't no big deal."

The door gunner laughed and returned to his searching scan out the open door. "Yellow just went up at 9 o'clock." He tersely reported.

The words were barely out of his mouth when the helicopter banked sharply to the left and began a swirling steep descent to the source of the yellow smoke. There was a PBR pulled up against the riverbank just yards from where the Huey sat down. Two men jumped from the boat and ran to the helicopter door and were pulled in by the crew chief as the door gunner stared into the nearby grass. They quickly clambered into place on the rear bench seat.

The crew chief yelled, "Clear!" as the pilot looked back around at his passengers.

"We're out'ta here." He drawled. As he pulled and twisted the collective handle, the helicopter quickly lifted from the riverbank. Pushing the cyclic stick forward, the main rotor was brushing through the grass as the machine pitched forward slighty. He stayed clear of the river as they accelerated away from the boat that was already pulling back out into the small tributary of the Saigon river. It too would quickly disappear as it headed back upriver – back toward Cambodia.

Smitty turned his head slightly towards the passengers and said, "Y'all buckle up, this is going to be a quick ride and it may get a little rough." He looked forward for a moment then turned back to the naval officer who was buckling himself in, "Templeton - How many times am I going to have to save your honky, white ass anyways?"

"Smitty, we're bingo in … 17 minutes.", said the co-pilot, somewhat nervously – again. Smitty gave him a quick, grimacing stare. "Shut up! Can't you see you're scaring our passengers?"

The gunner chimed in with, "The hell with the passengers, he's scaring the shit out of me!" Then he smiled and started them in on another refrain of 'Bingo'.

~

The soldiers in the nearby jungle had heard the unmistakable 'thumping' of the double bladed Huey as it banked sharply during the take off. They tried to get out from beneath the thick canopy of the trees they were in to fire on it. But only caught a glimpse of the helicopter through the trees as it raced overhead, unable to get off any shots at it. They saw the nose markings - a painted picture of the 'Grim

Reaper' - scythe and all. It was done up in black as well as the words beneath it, 'Black Death.' They had seen this bird before ...eventually they'd bring it down.

~ About the Author ~

Being not only the author, but the editor and self-publisher of Sycamore Glen and Sycamore Mill, I find it impossible to write about myself in the third person to inform you, the reader, of my background. What might qualify me to ask you to purchase my work and perhaps spend several evenings to immerse yourself in the world of Sycamore Glen?

I'm retired from a satisfying engineering career essentially as a designer of air conditioning equipment and similar mechanical work in other fields. I've been awarded several patents for ideas I've had that provided solutions to problems my employers presented me with. I have a wide variety of interests including woodworking and photography, as well as a love for the game of golf.

Being an avid reader, as is my wife, I've often thought I could put together an interesting story - at least for her and myself as a test of my abilities. Approaching the task of writing a novel is unlike anything I've ever been involved with. engineering work tends to be an organized, structured effort with milestones and defined end goals. My writing process is far from that. Even minor references to events or historical figures have led to tangential research that I would have never otherwise gotten into.

Most of Sycamore Glen, a story that precedes Sycamore Mill, poured out of me in a short, three-week period, during the summer of 2016. Over the next several months I refined the story in several places after having a small group of relatives and friends read the story as I continued to make minor changes to it.

Sycamore Mill, on the other hand, has taken much more time to write. I made a conscious decision to not 'recreate' the Sycamore Glen story. I wanted to try a more challenging approach to telling a story – hence the dual timelines of events. While I've been an avid reader of Civil War material, I've had to do research in areas of the war that I didn't really know much about. My wife and I have also visited several of the battlefields to get a 'feel' for the locations I'm writing about.

I've also had to delve into the world of self-publishing to be able to print and distribute the novels. I hope you can look past any minor technical errors I may have committed in my writing and in my editing, that full-time editors and publishers would have found and corrected.

Thank you for reading my story.

Brad Leech – November 2020

327

www.ingramcontent.com/pod-product-compliance
Lightning Source LLC
Chambersburg PA
CBHW031133160426
43193CB00008B/125